Mini Lop Ra

Mini Lop Rabbits as pets

Mini Lop Rabbit book for pros and cons, care, housing, cost, diet and health.

By

Macy Peterson

Table of Contents

Introduction

I want to thank you and congratulate you for buying this book. This book will help you to understand everything you need to know about domesticating a Mini lop rabbit. You will learn all the aspects related to raising the Mini lop rabbit successfully at home. You will be able to understand the pros and cons, behavior, basic care, keeping, housing, diet and health related to the animal.

There are people who are impressed by the adorable looks of the Mini lop rabbit. They think that this reason is enough to domesticate the animal, but the domestication of a mini lop rabbit has its unique challenges and issues. If you are not ready for these challenges, then you are not ready to domesticate the animal. If you have already bought or adopted a Mini lop rabbit, even then you need to understand your pet so that you take care of him or her in a better way. It is important that you understand that owning any pet will have its advantages and disadvantages.

You should see whether with all its pros and cons, the animal fits well into your household. Domesticating and taming a pet is not only fun, there is a lot of hard work that goes into it. It is important that you are ready to commit before you decide to domesticate the animal. If you are a prospective buyer, understanding these points will help you to make a wise decision. When you decide to hand raise a Mini lop rabbit, you will be flooded with questions in your head. Would I be able to care for him? Would I be able to domesticate a wild animal? What if I fail in my endeavor? You will find yourself thinking about these and many such questions.

Not matter how scared you are, you can always make it work if you equip yourself with the right knowledge. If you understand how a Mini lop rabbit should be cared for, you will make it work for yourself. You should make all possible efforts to understand the basic requirements of your pet. There are a few basic requirements that you will have to fulfill. Even if you can't afford to give the pet too much luxury, you should be able to take care of his basic requirements.

If you wish to raise a Mini lop rabbit as a pet, there are many things that you need to keep in mind. It can get very daunting for a new owner. Because of the lack of information, you will find yourself getting confused as to what should be done and what should be avoided. You might be confused and scared, but there is no need to feel so confused.

Once you form a relationship with the Mini lop rabbit, it gets better and easier for you as the owner. The pet will grow up to be friendly and adorable. He/she will also value the bond as much as you do. This will be good for the pet and also for you as the pet owner in the long run.

Chapter 1: Understanding a Mini lop rabbit

The mini lop rabbits belong to the medium sized class of rabbits. There are many species of medium and small sized rabbits. One of the characteristic features of these rabbits is that they have pendulous ears.

It should be noted that this species of rabbit is said to resemble the dwarfed lop rabbit. These rabbits are also small in size. They are very compact and tiny. The adult mature body weighs up to five pounds.

It is known that these rabbits are very gentle and friendly in their demeanour. They are attractive and playful in nature. These rabbits are available in many colours. This is an advantage for people looking for a colour of their choice.

There are many breeds of rabbits all over the world. The ARBA, which is the American Rabbit Breeders' Association, has already recognised over forty eight breeds of rabbits. On the other hand, the BRC, which is the British Rabbit Council, recognises over sixty breeds of rabbits.

It should be noted here that there could be several more breeds of rabbits that are still not recognised by the ARBA or BRC. There are many lop rabbit breeds amongst the rabbits. The mini lop is one these breeds.

Of all the breeds that are recognised all over the world, there are over nineteen breeds of lop rabbits. The term lop is used to describe a special type of ear in the rabbits. There are many breeds that are grouped together under the lop rabbit breeds.

It should be noted here that the deciding common factor amongst the lop rabbits is the shape of the ear. The various breeds grouped under the lop rabbits can differ in various parameters, such as colour and fur.

1. What are lop rabbits?

It should be noted that lop rabbits are not a specific breed of rabbits. It is only a certain kind and type of rabbit. There are further many breeds under this category. Any rabbit, irrespective of its breed, which has ears hanging from the head is called a lop rabbit.

Most rabbit breeds have ears that stand up straight. The ears are mostly small in size. The lop rabbit will have ears hanging from the side of the head. They look like little bells hanging from the head of the animal.

Lop rabbits can also be called lop eared rabbits. Lop rabbits are known to be friendly and cuddly by nature. But they require a lot of attention from your side. Any person who is not ready for the huge responsibility should not get a lop rabbit. They will require a lot of time and care from your side.

If you have the time and the energy to look after the lop rabbits, they can prove to be great pets. It has been stated earlier that there are over nineteen breeds of lop rabbits. It should be noted here that not all of them are recognised by the ARBA and the BRC.

In the United States, the ARBA recognised five breeds of lop rabbits. On the other hand, the BRC recognises nine breeds of lop eared rabbits.

The five breeds of lop rabbits recognised by the ARBA are American fuzzy lop, English lop, French lop, Holland lop and Miniature lop. The nine breeds of lop eared rabbits recognised by the BRC are the Cashmere lop, Cashmere miniature lop, English lop, German lop, Dwarf lop, French lop, Meissner lop, Miniature lion lop and Miniature lop.

There are different ways to differentiate between various lop eared rabbits. One of the most common ways to do so is to take the fur type into consideration. There are many rabbits that have velvety and short fur.

There are some rabbits which have long fur. A rabbit can also have medium type of fur. You can also use the shape of the rabbit as a parameter to distinguish between the various breeds of the same type.

Rabbits can also be categorised by the purpose they serve. Based on this criteria, there are three main types of rabbits, wool, meat and fur. The breeds that serve different purposes differ from each other in the way they look.

It is known that the breeds of rabbit meant for meat grow very quickly. They are large in their appearance. Such rabbits attain maturity by the age of eight to twelve weeks. They are ready to be used as meat by this time.

There are certain breeds of rabbits that are bred because of the quality of their fur. This fur is further used for clothes and coats. There are certain fur rabbits that are also meat rabbits. There are other types that are very popular for their wool.

2. What is a mini lop rabbit?

The mini lop rabbit is a very popular breed of domestic rabbits which is found in United States of America. If you see the smallest of rabbits in the lop eared rabbits category, mini lop rabbit is the third smallest of them all.

The mini lop rabbit is also known to be the smallest of the non dwarfed lop rabbits. It should be known here that the mini lop rabbits are known as dwarf lops in the United Kingdom, though they are not really dwarfed.

The mini lop rabbit is a small rabbit which has lopped ears, hence the name 'mini lop'. It should also be noted here that in the United Kingdom, there is a very popular breed of domestic rabbits that are called miniature lops. These are not mini lop rabbits.

This particular breed was developed in Germany. This was done in the second half of the twentieth century. The mini lop rabbit was found in the United States for the first time in the year 1974.

These bunnies have hanging ears, hence the name lop ears. A small rabbit which has ears hanging from the side of the head is said to be a mini lop rabbit. They are popular for their intelligence and their playful and friendly demeanour.

The rabbit stays small its entire life. This makes it ideal for people that do not have much space in their house but still wish to pet a rabbit. It can make an ideal pet if you can give your time and attention to the mini lop rabbit.

If you are a prospective owner of the mini lop rabbit then this section will help you to learn more about the mini lop rabbit. You will learn some interesting facts about the mini lop rabbit.

The mini lop rabbit is called mini, but they are classified under medium sized rabbits. They do not grow too big in size. The mini lop rabbit has been nicknamed, 'basketball with a head'. This is in tune with the body structure of the animal.

3. History of mini lop rabbits

The mini lop rabbit was discovered by Bon Herschbach in the year 1972. He is also credited with naming the rabbits 'mini lop rabbit'. This breed is a cross between two other popular breeds, the Chinchilla and the German big lop. In the early times, the mini lop was only found in the colors white and agouti. This is because the Chinchilla and the German big lop were found only in these two colors.

Bon Herschbach brought the mini lop rabbits from Germany to the United States. In USA, he started breeding these animals on his own. The first generation is said to have very solid colors. The second generation is said to have exhibited broken colors. He introduced the mini lop rabbits to the ARBA in one of their conventions.

The sponsorship of the mini lop rabbit was then transferred. A club was started, which became popular within a year or so. In 1980, ARBA made the mini lop rabbit an official breed.

4. Body structure

Mini lop rabbits are very small in size. They are in fact amongst the smallest of rabbits. The mini lop rabbit has a compact body and curved profile and its legs are short and rounded.

The head is round in shape. The head and eyes are bigger in comparison to the body. The ears have a peculiar shape and are erect. The structure of the ears helps the rabbit to protect itself from many bacteria and infections.

The coat of the mini lop rabbit is thick, dense and soft. The rabbit comes in different coat colors such as black, white, blue, chocolate, lilac, fox, tortoiseshell, sable marten, siamese sable, chestnut, agouti, siamese smoke pearl, fawn, sable point, himalayan, steel, lynx, broken pattern opal, tan, squirrel, chinchilla, otter, orange, silver marten and smoke pearl marten.

They have wide shoulders, deep chests and loins. The ears of the mini lop rabbits are very close to his chest. They hang approximately one inch below the jaw and are round near the area of the ears. There are folds in the ears of the mini lop rabbit.

It should be noted that these folds of the ears should not be thin or very thick. When you inspect a mini lop rabbit, this is the first thing that you should be inspecting. If you are keeping the rabbit with a criterion to attend shows then this is important, otherwise it is fine.

The small size of the rabbit makes it ideal as a pet and also as an exhibition animal. However, this small size also constricts its use as a primary source of fur and meat.

5. Size and weight

The body of a mini lop is well muscled and well balanced. The coat is thick and dense. The maximum weight attained by a mini lop rabbit has been defined by the ARBA and the BRC. According to the ARBA, the maximum weight attained by the mini lop is 6.5 pounds. According to the BRC, the maximum weight gained by the mini lop rabbit is 5 pounds.

6. Life span of mini lop rabbits

A healthy mini lop rabbit can live from 7 to over 10 years. It is known that a rabbit that is cared for and groomed in a good way and that is kept indoors will have a good life span.

The key is to provide them the right environment and also the right nutrition. This will help them to grow, stay healthy and live longer.

7. Mini lop rabbit colors

As stated earlier, the mini lop rabbits are available in many colors. This gives the rabbit lover a chance to choose from his favourite colors. This section will help you understand the colors and patterns that your mini lop rabbit can come in.

Self

The self-colored type refers to the rabbit that has a single color all over the body. This means that a single color will be seen on the body, limbs, head and ears of the animal. The various colors in this pattern are white, blue, chocolate and black.

Agouti

This pattern has typically three or even more colors. There is a dark base color and alternating colors run through the base color. The top of the rabbit and the side of the rabbit are said to be ticked and banded. You will notice that the tip of various hairs is of a different color. The various colors in this pattern include chestnut, opal and chinchilla.

Shaded

In this type, there is a main color. There is a gradual change from this main color, as the shade keeps getting lighter. The sides and belly typically have

10

the lighter shade of color. The various colors in this pattern include sable medium, sable light, smoke pearl and chocolate point.

Broken

This is one of the most common categories in the mini lop rabbits. A mini lop rabbit is said to belong to the broken color category when the rabbit has a combination of two colors, white color and any other color.

The color of the body of the rabbit is broken in an even pattern. There is color around the eyes and ears of the rabbit and also around the nose. The mini lops exhibiting this pattern are also called broken lops.

The color possessed by the broken lops is anywhere between ten percent and seventy percent. Generally, there is a marking on the nose which is called the butterfly marking. This marking is outlined by the color white.

The circles around the ears and the eyes are of a different color. It is also seen that the front feet of the mini lop are white. The back feet may be colored or may also be white. These are some of the general characteristics of the broken category in the mini lop rabbits.

Ticked

This is another category of the mini lop rabbits. A mini lop rabbit belongs to this category if the tips of its hairs are of a different colour to the color of its body. It is said that the bunnies in the ticked category have the steel gene.

These rabbits can possess ticking in silver or in gold. If you wish to know the colors that this category holds, then you should know that you can get a mini lop bunny in smoke, sable, silver fox, lilac, chocolate, blue and also black.

Wide band

A mini lop rabbit with the wide band will look quite similar to the one in the agouti category. But, there are a couple of differences that separate the two patterns. While the secondary color shows around the ears, tail and eyes in the agouti, it shows in a layer in the wide band pattern.

A mini lop rabbit belonging to this particular category will have a particular color at the top. There will be another color at the bottom part of the bunny's body.

The colors that you can expect to find in the white band category are fawn, orange, red, frosty and cream.

8. Pros and cons of keeping mini lop rabbits

If you wish to hand raise an animal, you should make sure that you understand the characteristics and the requirements of the animal. When you domesticate the mini lop rabbit, you will face many pros and cons along the way.

This section will help you understand the pros and cons of keeping a mini lop rabbit at home.

Pros of keeping a mini lop rabbit at home

There are many pros of keeping a mini lop rabbit:

- These rabbits enjoy the company of human beings and are known to have a good time with them.

- These pets are great for smaller living spaces, such as a flat or small house.

- These pets are generally low maintenance. They do not need frequent baths, which can be a great relief for a caregiver.

- A rabbit is a very intelligent and smart animal. You can easily train him/her to suit your family and living conditions.

- The rabbit is beautiful to look at. If you are fond of beautiful looking pets, then this rabbit is definitely the pet for you and your family.

- The rabbits are very energetic and lively pets. They are very active during the early hours of the morning and evening.

- The rabbits are very sweet, entertaining and gentle in their nature, yet they need to be trained well so that they don't get too mischievous. You will also get to see the calm, composed and gentle side of the animal.

- If they are raised to be social, they will be very social. You should make sure that they spend a lot of time indoors with the family members. This will only help in being more social and affectionate.

- The rabbit is a very playful, happy-go-lucky kind of animal. The rabbit likes having fun and can be a constant source of entertainment for everyone in the family.

- You can enter your pet in various shows that happen everywhere. These are shows that can help you gain popularity and can help you win also.

- They are capable of forming strong emotional bonds. These bonds will last for a lifetime. You need to spend quality time with your pet to form such strong bonds.

- You will find it easier to groom the pet because he/she will be relaxed and calm, unlike many other pets that don't allow the owners to groom them.

- It has been established over the years that the rabbits are easy to train.

- When you domesticate a rabbit, you will have to worry less about diet. This is because nowadays many diet mixtures and pellets are available commercially. These food items ensure that the right nutrition is given to your beloved pet. You can be happy because you can save yourself from the tension of preparing food mixes for the pet every now and then.

- You will have to be extra careful and cautious while taking care of the kit, but when all the precautions are taken, it is a very much possible task to hand raise a bunny or kit.

- They will respond to the way you choose to communicate with them. If you provide good training to your rabbit, you will notice that he/she responds well. In due time and over the course of the training, the pet will also start obeying some simple commands that you want them to obey.

Cons of keeping a mini lop rabbit at home

There are many cons of keeping a mini lop rabbit:

- The mini lop rabbit can get nervous and frightened very easily. They can get uneasy and can slip into depression if not looked after.

- These rabbits enjoy the company of human beings and are known to have a good time with them. But, they should be trained to socialize from an early age. If they don't socialize from the beginning, they can develop aggression towards human beings and other animals.

- Bigger animals can make the mini lop rabbit prey.

- You can't keep these animals in a cage at all times. They need space and time to explore and play.

- If the rabbit is not under supervision, it can get very mischievous. The animal will chew things; even electrical wiring.

- The pet is also prone to many diseases. The caregiver will have to be very careful with the health of the pet.

- The pet can get stressed and depressed if it is left lonely for long durations. You can't leave it in the cage for too long.

- The bunnies love to dig in the ground. In fact, the rabbit will try to dig everywhere. If the pet is left on its own, it might try to dig in your sofas, beds, etc.

- If you don't have the time and energy to spend on grooming a pet, then the mini lop rabbit is not the right pet for you.

- If the children of the house are not careful, they can scare the pet. This can be detrimental to the mini lop rabbit.

- The cost that you will incur while buying and raising is more when compared to other pets, such as the dog and the cat. If spending too much money is an issue with you, then you will have to think twice before purchasing the animal.

- These animals love playing and running around. These pets are fond of exploring things and can create a mess if not monitored.

Chapter 2: Things to know before you buy a mini lop rabbit

Before you buy a mini lop rabbit and bring him home to hand raise him, it is important that you understand certain facts regarding these animals. (Please note that although you can have females, we shall refer to them as 'he' for ease). You should understand their behavior and also the cost incurred in domesticating them. Having knowledge of all these things will help you to make a better decision regarding the domestication of the mini lop rabbit.

1. Are you ready for a mini lop rabbit?

Mini lop rabbits will require lots of love and attention from your side. You will have to dedicate time for their grooming and also general care. You should also take out time to spend quality time with them.

If you are worried whether the bunny will be able to form emotional bonds in your home or not, then you shouldn't worry too much about it. If you focus on the right things and the rest will only follow.

You will be surprised to see how loyal and friendly your pet will be towards you. The pet will grow up to be friendly and affectionate. You can also form a good bond with the pet animal.

Like with other pets, once you form a personal bond with the bunny, it gets better and easier for you as the owner. If you get a young bunny home and spend your time and energy to raise him, you will notice as the animal grows older, it gets very fond of you.

The mini lop rabbit is an animal that is known to have loads of energy. This will make him an active pet. You should lay emphasis on the quality of time you give to be with your bunny.

As the animal grows, he will value the bond that will be formed between the two of you. It is important that you make the right efforts for this bond to be formed between the bunny and you.

When you decide to domesticate an animal, it is more than important that you are prepared to solve the issues that might arise. You should be well equipped to do the same. Any animal will have certain requirements that you would have to fulfil if you wish to hand raise the animal.

The foremost concern of a prospective owner should always be to give the pet an environment that helps him to live happily. The pet should be able to grow and dwell in a healthy environment.

It is also important that you understand the licensing requirements of your area before you decide to domesticate the animal. This will help you avoid any legal hassles in the future regarding the domestication of the pet.

You should make all necessary arrangements to make sure that you provide the pet with all the necessities of food and shelter. This chapter will help you to understand the basic needs and requirements of your mini lop rabbit. This will help you make all the necessary arrangements to domesticate the animal.

If you have other pets, such as cats and dogs in the house, then this could be a very important concern for you. If you are looking to get a new rabbit then also the compatibility issues between the pet and the rabbit would be on the top of your mind.

It is important that the pets in the house get along with each other. This will make the atmosphere of the house very lively. You should look for the reactions that the pets have when they are with each other.

If the pets don't gel with each other, then it is not good for all the animals. As the owner, things will get difficult for you also because the primary concern of the owner is to give protection and safety to the pets.

You might have to keep them separate to make sure that everything in the house is fine. This is fine as long as they are not disturbing each other.

It is important that you understand the various criteria that will affect the compatibility of various pets with each other. These criteria will be of the temperament of the animals and also their age.

Sometimes, the animals don't intend to harm each other. But, they don't know how to behave with each other. In this confusion, they can end up harming each other.

So, as the owner you have to be on guard to make sure that all the animals are safe and none are harmed.

2. Costs that you will incur

As a prospective owner, you might be wondering about the costs that you need to be prepared for to domesticate the mini lop rabbit. As the owner and parent of the pet, you will have to make attempts to fulfil all the needs of the animal. You should also be prepared on the financial front to take care of these needs.

It is better that you plan these things well in advance. This planning will help you to avoid any kind of disappointment that you might face when there are some payments that need to be made.

There are basically two kinds of costs that you will be looking to incur, which are as follows:

- **The one-time costs**: The one-time costs are the ones that you will have to bear in the beginning when you decide hand raise a mini lop rabbit. This will include the one-time payment that you will give to buy the animal. There are other purchases that would come under this category, such as the permits and the license fee of the pet, purchasing price of food containers and the price of the enclosure.
- **The on-going costs**: The on-going costs are the ones that you will have to spend each month or once every few months to raise the mini lop rabbit. This category includes the costs of the food requirements and health requirements of the pet.

You should work out all these things right in the beginning, so that you don't suffer any problems later. Realizing at a later stage that you can't keep the animal and giving it up is never a good idea. You can maintain a journal to keep track of the costs.

Cost of a mini lop rabbit

The price of the mini lop rabbit will depend on where you choose to buy the mini lop rabbit from. You can get a rescued rabbit from a rescue centre or animal shelter, if it is available.

The next choice is to buy one from the breeder. The cost will vary depending on the quality of the mini lop rabbit. A very good quality mini lop rabbit bought from a top class breeder will cost you around $80/£58.06.

Depending on your choice of breeder and the choice of mini lop rabbit quality, you can expect to spend $20/£14.52 to $100/£72.58 for buying the bunny.

Health costs

It is important to include the cost of healthcare when working on various costs for the pet mini lop. This will help you to get an idea on what you can expect to spend on the general keeping of the pet mini lop rabbit.

The mini lop rabbit does require shots and vaccinations, so you need to spend money on the vaccinations. You can expect to spend $80/£58.06 on both the important vaccines.

The only regular medication that the mini lops need is the commercial pellets. These pellets are required to keep the issue of wool block at bay. You can expect to spend about $10/£7.65 on 600 of these tablets.

These tablets don't need to be given daily. They can be given twice or thrice a week, so that means 600 tablets will last you a very long time.

You would be relieved to know that the mini lop rabbit does not get sick that often. If you take care of the food and hygiene of the bunny, you can save him from many diseases. He will lead a healthy life if you take the necessary precautions.

You should always focus on the health of the mini lop rabbit. This is necessary because an unhealthy animal is the breeding ground of many other diseases in the home. Your pet might pass on the diseases to other pets if not treated on time.

The rabbit will not fall sick that often, but you should bring your pet to the veterinarian for regular check-ups. This is to avoid any future health problems.

You should also be prepared for unexpected costs, such as sudden illness or accident of the mini lop rabbit. Health care is provided at different prices in different areas. So, the veterinarian in your area could be costlier than the veterinarian in the nearby town.

Cost of food

A domesticated mini lop rabbit will mostly be fed hay, grass and vegetables. You might also have to include various pellets and supplements to give your pet overall nourishment. It is important that you understand the food requirements of your mini lop in the beginning, so that you can be prepared on the monetary front.

You should feed about two cups of greens per day to the rabbit. This should cost you around $10/£7.68 per month. You can expect to pay $3/£2.32 to $5/£3.84 for the pellets.

You should make sure that there is enough fibre in the diet of the mini lop rabbit. You need to feed timothy hay to the mini lop rabbit every day. This should cost you about $3/£2.32 per month.

Cost of hygiene

A pet needs to be clean and hygienic. If you fail at maintaining hygiene levels for your pet, it will only lead to other complications. The basic hygiene of the pet can be maintained by a good quality shampoo and some towels.

There are many owners that insist on litter training. If you too wish to litter train your pet mini lop rabbit, you will have to buy the required products for the same. You would need to buy paper litter for the bunny because it is safe even when the rabbit ingests it.

You will also be required to invest in a good detergent, which could be bleach. This will be needed to clean the cage and all the areas where the mini lop rabbit might defecate.

This is a very basic amount that you will have to encounter. You should invest in some good cleaning products and sanitizers.

You can look at spending \$4/£3.07 for the paper litter per month for the pet. The other requirements of shampoo and detergents should not cost you more than \$10/£7.66 per month.

Cost of rabbit cage

The shelter of the animal will be his home, so it is important that you construct the shelter according to the animal's needs. If the pet is not indoors, then most likely he will be in his cage. So, it is important to make this one time investment in a way that is best for the mini lop rabbit.

The cage of the mini lop rabbit should be six feet long, two feet wide and two feet deep. If you can provide extra space to the mini lop, it is better. The price of shelter will depend on the type of the shelter. You can expect to spend \$10/£7.66 to \$20/£15.36 for the cage.

Miscellaneous costs

Although the main costs that you will encounter while raising your pet have already been discussed, there will be some extra things that you will have to take care of. Most of these are one-time costs only.

You will have to spend money to buy stuff such as a grooming comb, litter box, scissors, brush, nail clippers, feed bin, water bottle, accessories and toys for the pet. If you think that something needs to be repaired or replaced, you will have to spend money on doing that.

You can expect to spend some $100/£76.58 on these things. The exact amount will depend on the wear and tear and the quality of the products. In order to keep track of things, you should regularly check the various items in the cage or hutch of the pet bunny.

3. Mini lop rabbit vaccination

It is important to get the mini lop rabbit vaccinated. You should get the bunny vaccinated against myxomatosis and RVHD (Rabbit viral haemorrhagic disease). You will need to give the bunny two vaccines per year to protect him against these two diseases.

If you are in UK, then The Rural Land Protection Act of 1989 makes it compulsory to vaccinate the rabbit with fibroma vaccine. The veterinarian might also advise the caregivers to give the mini lop rabbits a vaccine against Calcivirus.

4. Mini lop rabbit insurance

You can get insurance for your mini lop rabbit. This insurance will help you to take care of the veterinarian bills and injury costs. Though the mini lop rabbit does not get sick easily, a sudden procedure can cost you over thousands of pounds/dollars.

If you buy insurance to cover these conditions, you will save yourself from a lot of trouble. Depending on the insurance you buy, you can also cover regular clinic visits. There are some companies that will give you discounts on clinic visits.

There are some companies that can help you with mini lop rabbit insurance, such as Exotic direct, Pet Plan, Helpucover and NCI. These companies have different kinds of insurance. You can choose according to your requirement. You can also get a package deal if you are looking to insure more than one mini lop rabbit.

When you buy insurance, you have to pay a deductible amount and regular premiums. You will also be required to pay premiums that need to be paid regularly to keep the insurance policy active.

Rabbit insurance can cost you around $8/£6.14 to $20/£15.35 per month. The exact amount will depend on the company that you choose and also on the area that you live in.

5. Neutering or spaying

Neutering or spaying has become an important part of pet domestication. As an owner, you need to make a decision whether you would want your pets to have progenies or not.

Mini lop rabbits can be neutered or spayed by the owners or the breeders. When you are sure that you don't want your doe to breed, it is better to spay the animal before it is too late. Similarly, neuter the male if you don't want breeding.

It should also be understood that neutering or spaying the rabbit will have its consequences on the pet. It is better to understand these consequences. Talk to the veterinarian about them and be prepared for them.

It is known that males get less aggressive if they are neutered at the right age. It is advised to get the process done before it is four months old. If the rabbit is an adult, neutering or spaying will have a lot of complications, which you would definitely want to avoid.

The sexual organs of the rabbits are located towards the inside and the animal is also very small. The entire process can be very tricky and complicated. It is extremely important that you get the neutering or spaying done by a trained professional who has experience dealing with these animals.

6. Breeding in mini lop rabbits

As a new or prospective owner of a mini lop rabbit, you might be interested in the breeding cycle and procedure of the mini lop rabbits. Breeding is defined as the process of production of an offspring by mating of the male and the female adults.

This chapter is meant to clear all your doubts regarding the breeding of mini lop rabbits. It is important to understand the breeding patterns of your pet animals. How well you understand the mating patterns of your pet will also determine how well you look after the pet.

There are many owners who are interested in rabbit breeding and production of the younger ones. The breeding in a controlled environment at your house can be challenging. But, it will get easier to understand once you equip yourself with all the right knowledge.

It is also known that the mother can sometimes kill the kits one after the other. There are many reasons behind this. The mother might do it when she is unable to provide nutrition to the kit.

If the kit has a danger of predators, such as wild dogs, even then the mother might decide to kill the kits. It is important that the mother rabbit is kept under observation during her nesting phase.

If your female rabbits tend to kill its young ones, you will have to keep the little ones away from her. It is known that if the mother kills more than two of her kits, she should not be allowed to breed again.

Mating behaviour of the mini lop rabbits

You should understand the natural mating behaviour of your mini lops. This will help you to do the right thing while breeding them. This chapter is meant to equip you with all the knowledge that you might need while mating your rabbits.

Each animal species has their unique breeding habits and patterns. When you are looking to take care of your pet well, you should also lay enough emphasis on understanding its breeding patterns.

The male mini lop rabbit gets sexually mature at the age of seven to eight months, while the female mini lop rabbits get sexually mature a month earlier, which is six to seven months of age.

It should also be noted that the different breeds of mini lops differ slightly in the time by which the males and females reach sexual maturity.

The younger mini lop rabbits are referred to as bunnies or kits. A female mini lop is able to produce many kits at a single time. These rabbits are known to be very active sexually. Anyone looking to breed rabbits and produce kits will not be disappointed.

It should be understood that rabbits are able to follow one mating cycle with the other in short durations of time. This means that if the mating procedure of the mini lop rabbits is not understood and controlled, your house could be flooded with kits.

A good breeder will always encourage you to thoroughly understand the sexual tendencies of your rabbits, so as to not commit any mistake in the future. You need to know how often and in what conditions your rabbits can reproduce.

In the wild, the kits have higher chances of survival in a warm environment. This means that the rabbits enter their mating cycle in warmer temperatures. You can expect the same when the rabbits are domesticated.

When a rabbit is in its natural environment, the extra amount of light during the summers and also spring brings about a change in its body. The male and female rabbits get sexually active during this time.

A male rabbit will display changes in its behaviour. It will seem more aggressive and restless. This is due to the sex hormones that have become active in its body. This is how you can identify if your male mini lop is ready to mate or not.

Another interesting behaviour that can be noted in the males is that they become more competitive with other male rabbits. The males that are sexually active compete with each other to establish dominance in the group. This is done so that they can impress the female and attract her for mating.

It is known that in the wild, the dominant male mini lops have a good sex life in comparison to the shy ones. When you see your pet male mini lop getting too aggressive and competitive, you should know that he is ready for mating.

When your male rabbit and female rabbit are ready for mating, you should bring the female rabbit to the male rabbit's cage. It should be noted that the opposite should not be done.

You should not take the male rabbit to the female rabbit's cage because the female rabbit can get territorial. You might find the female attacking and harming the male instead of mating with him.

Once the male rabbit (buck) is able to attract the female rabbit (doe), the mating can begin. During the process, the female will lie down on a level surface on the ground as an invitation to the male rabbit. The female will also lift its tail.

The male will mount himself on the female rabbit at this time. The male is known to cast a sharp bite on the nape of the female at this time. This process should last just over twenty seconds.

The mating process will end here and the male will release the female at this time. It should also be noted that the male rabbit will have fur in his mouth because of the bite he had cast. He will also lose his consciousness for some time after the entire process is over.

Now, the female is pregnant. The gestation period in the female will last for over a month. Once that is over, you can expect your pregnant mini lop to give birth to three to eight kits or bunnies.

It should be noted that the new born kits are hairless. They are also blind at this time. The female is capable of repeating the same process and giving birth to bunnies many times in a year.

Nesting

When you are conducting controlled mating at your home, then there are many things that you will have to take care of. You should make sure that the male and the female rabbit are in the same cage when they are both ready.

After they have mated, you should be ready to take care of the doe. It is also important that you take care of the nesting requirements of the rabbits once the mating is over and the female rabbit is pregnant.

The nesting box is a box that will be used by the female rabbit as the nest. She will give birth to the bunnies in the nest. You should make sure that the box is big enough to allow the rabbit to be comfortable. The young ones will spend a lot of time in the nesting box, so it should be as comfortable as possible.

You should only place the nesting box in the rabbit cage when the time is right. If you do it any earlier, the rabbit will try to dig it as if it is digging a burrow. The rabbit might also use the box as a litter box. Make sure that this does not happen.

The kindling are expected after one month of the female getting pregnant. So, you should ideally keep the nesting box in the cage of the rabbit on the 28th day after mating has taken place.

The female is expected to give birth anytime from the 28th day to the 31st day after mating. Of course, the mating should have been successful.

You should put some soft pine and hay in the nest box before keeping it in the cage of the rabbit. This will give a cushion-like structure to the nest. It will make the nest box cosy and comfortable.

There is a natural tendency of the female rabbit that is about give birth. She will pull out some hair from under her chin. This will be used by her as a cushion for the young ones that are to arrive.

The doe will use this nesting box to give birth to the young ones. Initially, the young ones will spend all their time in the box. This is because they will be too small to come out of the nesting box.

After the female rabbit gives birth to the bunnies in the nest, she will try to spend most of the time outside the nest. You will see her in the cage, but outside the nest box. The mother will get into the cage to feed the young ones. You can expect this to happen at least twice a day.

After three weeks, you will see that the young ones have started coming out of the nest. They will keep hopping in and out of the nest box at this time.

When you notice that the bunnies are spending a good amount of time outside the box, you should remove the box. The kits don't need it anymore.

Raising a baby rabbit

When bring get a pet home, it is more like a new member of the family. It is very important that you take time to understand the various stages in the pet's life. Each stage will demand different care and methods.

In case you decide to breed your mini lop rabbit, you will face the situation where you will have to take care of a kit. There are many people who buy kits from the breeders. They also have to face the same situation.

Hand rearing a baby rabbit can be very tricky, but if you pay attention to the details, it will be fun and interesting. You should take care of a few things to make sure that your baby rabbit is taken care of.

When a baby rabbit or kit is born, he has no hair. He is also blind and deaf. You shouldn't be too surprised to see this condition. You can expect the kit to get his first hairs after a few days of his birth.

The kit will open his eyes approximately ten days after its birth. This is the time when the ears of the kit also start to open.

It should also be noted that body temperature regulation is very important for a mini lop rabbit. But, a baby rabbit is unable to regulate the temperature of his body. It is only after 7-8 days that you can expect him to do so.

Breeding in mini lop rabbits can happen after the doe gives birth to the babies. People who breed rabbits for wool generally wait for 40-42 days before they rebreed.

The female rabbit will give birth to about twelve kits at a time. Some can even give birth to more. A female rabbit will have about eight to ten nipples. This makes it easier for her to feed all her kits.

If a mother is not capable of taking care of the young one, then the kits can be given to another female rabbit that is in the same age group as the mother.

This should be done in the first few days of kindling, preferably the first three days.

The kits are weaned after about five weeks of their birth. Even when they are feeding off the mother, they need to do it twice a day. Each feed time will last for about three to four minutes.

You need to be well prepared when you hand rear an infant. It can be very challenging if you don't get your basics right. You should make sure that you do the right things for the kit.

While you might have learnt it all, there are a few important points that need to be remembered when taking care of the infant mini lop rabbit. You will have to be patient with your pet infant. This is the key.

Try to understand the position of a new born and never force him for anything. Just try to give him a warm and secure environment. This is very important.

If you are hand raising the infant rabbit, then you need to substitute the mother rabbit's milk. This can be easily done.

When you feed the milk formula to the baby rabbit, you should make sure that the milk is at the temperature of the blood of the infant. This is a very important point. There is a simple formula for the feed that you should be giving your infant bunny.

Take half cup of water, half a cup of evaporated milk, one tsp. of corn starch and one egg yolk and mix everything together. One tablespoon of this formula should be given once or twice in a day.

The kits will start eating green leaves and grass after fifteen to twenty days of their birth. You can introduce the greens to them at this time along with the milk formula. This will take care of their daily nutritional requirement.

It is important to note that the infant of the rabbit has absolutely no way of keeping itself warm for the first week after its birth. It can't regulate its temperature, yet it should be kept warm to keep it safe.

You will have to make sure that the baby rabbit is experiencing the right temperatures. He has to be warm at all times. But, make sure that the temperature does not get too hot. This can also be harmful for the rabbit.

Before you can start feeding your kit, wrap the infant safely in a blanket. This will help to keep the infant warm. You will have to constantly monitor the temperature so that it does not over-heat the infant.

You should keep the infant cl(
warmth is also important for th(
him with the bottle, try to keep t
your body in your lap.

You can try opening the mouth of
finger and thumb. Make sure that you

You can also close his eyes with your
These are simple tricks that can help you
cooperative.

It might take some time, but the infant rab
time. You will see him being more comfort   ...u should
be a little patient and kind with the rabbit.

Another important point that you need to know is that the bottle being used
to feed the baby rabbit should never be squeezed when the nipples are in the
baby's mouth. The infant is still learning. The infant's body is still
developing.

When you squeeze the bottle, there could be a rush of milk inside the
infant's body. The liquid could even enter the baby's lungs. So, the best way
is to let the animal drink at his pace.

The initial phase of trying to nurse the infant can be stressful and challenging
for you. But slowly as the days progress, things will get easier. It has been
noticed with the infant rabbits that they might take some time to get used to
you and the new surroundings.

But, once the infant gets used to you and the environment, you will have a
great emotional bond with them. The nursing time will also become easier
and also memorable.

If your infant is rejecting the milk or the milk formula that is being served to
him, then there could be another reason than him being uncomfortable in the
new surroundings. It is possible that the animal is rejecting it because he
feels unsafe.

You should make sure that the water you use to prepare the formula has been
cooled after heating it. It should be noted that you should not use cold water
because it is not right for the formula.

You should also not use boiling water because it can again destroy the
mineral content of the formula. A simple way to make use of the water is to
boil the water, and then let the boiled water cool down.

rabbit, he might resist the feed or might just
is normal behaviour by the kit and you should
on't force him. Just gently keep trying and finally the
milk formula and also the feeding method.

that the young ones can be affected by bowel related diseases
diseases that directly affect the urinary tract. It will be difficult to
rol the infection once it starts spreading. The baby is too young to have
any immunity against such diseases.

It is important that you look for the first signs of infection. If you see something is wrong, you should make sure that you consult the vet as soon as possible.

While you are feeding the baby rabbit, you should be very particular about the hygiene of the baby and his surroundings. If there is any milk spillage, clean it immediately so that the area does not become a breeding place for diseases and infections.

In most cases of Mini lop rabbit domestication, people buy kits from a breeder. It becomes essential to understand the baby bunny and give him an environment that closely resembles to what it would have been if he was with to his mother.

There is also a probability that you have rescued the infant from the wild. If you have rescued a litter, then it becomes all the more that difficult for you. This is because the infant must be scared and you will have to work on him on an emotional level.

The baby rabbit could be trapped or could be in danger of predators. You will have to take into account the condition of the infant when you are making a plan of how to care for your bunny.

You should understand the baby mini lop rabbit will be very scared of all the new things coming its way. You have to be well prepared for this.

Be kind and have some empathy towards the baby. Even if it is difficult for you to see the scared kit, you need to be calm. The kit will get better with time and with the care you provide it.

Mini lop rabbits can grow up to be very good pets if they are loved and cared for in the beginning. This first year is a crucial time because this is when the kit forms intimate bonds with human beings.

The emotional bonds that it forms at this stage will stay with him for his whole life. He will be loyal towards them. Make sure that you pay as much attention to the development of the infant rabbit.

When the mini lop rabbit is very young, it is always advised to keep him under constant observation. He should be supervised by you at all times. Even if you are not around and are busy, then a family member should be around the rabbit.

You should also be careful when you are planning to start solid foods for the baby rabbit. Even though the baby rabbit is ready, you can't start giving him the adult food right away.

As the owner of a mini lop rabbit, you might be surrounded by many questions. It is important that you learn about the right time and the right ways to introduce solid food to the little one. The kit will enjoy its food as much as it enjoyed its milk.

You should start with the introduction of simpler solid foods in the baby mini lop rabbit's diet. This will help him to develop his digestive tract before he can start eating the real adult food of the mini lop rabbits.

7. Purchasing a mini lop rabbit

Once you have made up your mind whether you want to buy the mini lop rabbit or not, the next obvious step is to look for the right place to buy it. You can do so from a pet store or directly from a breeder.

Before you buy your mini lop rabbit, it is important that you do your research well. You should also have the right information about various pet stores and breeders in your area.

You can visit various pet stores to look for the kind of mini lop rabbit that you are looking for. The local veterinarian can give his/her recommendations in this case. It is always advisable to buy a mini lop rabbit from a reputable breeder.

The problem with pet stores is that you would not come to know about the history of the rabbit, which is so important to understand the health of the animal. You will also not be able to understand the breeding process and conditions of the animal. These are some important factors in determining the health and the history of the animal.

Buying a rabbit from a breeder has its many benefits. You can talk to the breeder about the many concerns that you might have. You can understand the breeding procedure of the animal and can also be sure that the animal has been in safe hands before you.

You should also make sure that you select the right breeder to buy the rabbit from. It is as important as buying the right pet. If you choose the wrong breeder, you will only have to face problems in the future.

It will pay to talk to other people who have bought rabbits in your region. They could help you in deciding on the right breeders.

There are some breeders who are in this profession for the love of mini lop rabbits and animals in general. Of course they wish to earn money, but not by compromising their prime duty as a breeder.

You will also find breeders who do this only for the sake of money. Such breeders will not hesitate in providing you with the wrong information about the rabbit to make a few bucks. You need to save yourself from such selfish breeders.

It is important that you devote some time in looking for breeders in and around your region. You should understand the reputation of the breeder before you choose him/her to buy your rabbit.

As the potential buyer, you should know every little detail about your pet animal. You need to make sure that the breeder you choose to buy the mini lop rabbit from shares all the details about the rabbit.

A good breeder will always ask you questions and will make sure that the animal will get a good owner and a good home. You can expect this from a breeder who cares enough for the animals that he/she keeps.

The breeder would want to understand the prime motive behind you buying the rabbit. He/she would also want to understand if you have the time and energy to devote to the rabbit. The mini lop rabbit can be demanding as a pet, and you should make sure that you can provide for it.

There have been cases where the breeders have denied permission to the prospective owners because they didn't seem able to provide well for the animal. So if your breeder is asking you questions about how you intend to keep the animal, then this is a good sign.

The breeder will also give you a set of instructions that will come in handy when you are taking care of the rabbit. You should make sure that you understand these instructions well.

List of websites

You also have the option of adopting a rabbit. There are some factors that will govern the final choice that you make. You should make sure that you understand these factors, so that you can make the right choice for yourself as the owner of a new pet.

Many rabbits are mistreated and abandoned by their owners. You can help to give one of these abandoned rabbits a new home. The abandoned rabbit will get a new home and your family will get a new pet.

If you want to buy a kit or younger rabbit, then you should buy him from a good breeder. If you are looking to bring an older rabbit to your home, then you should try to go for adoption.

If you are looking at the financial side of the deal, then you can benefit from adopting the rabbit. Many a times, you can expect to get a cage and other accessories with the abandoned rabbit. This will save you from building or buying a new cage for the animal.

Most adult mini lop rabbits are vaccinated and litter trained. They are also spayed or neutered. This will also help you to save some money.

Note: at the time of printing, all the websites below were working. As the internet changes rapidly, some sites might no longer be live when you read this book. That is, of course, out of our control.

If you are looking for reputed breeders, then the following list can help you:

- Rabbit haven: https://therabbithaven.org

- Bunnies are us: www.bunniesareus.com

- Dwarf R US: www. dwarfsrus.com

- Rabbit breeders: http://rabbitbreeders.us

- Evergreen farm: www.evergreenfarm.biz

- Friends of rabbits: www.friendsofrabbits.org

8. Do you need license to keep mini lop rabbits?

Once you are acquainted with the basic knowledge about the mini lop rabbits, the next important question is whether a license is needed to domesticate them. Before you can decide where you should buy the bunny, it is important to know about the licensing requirements.

It is important to understand the licensing rules of the mini lop rabbits. You should be sure that the law permits you to hand raise the animal. This is important because the law prohibits the domestication of certain animals.

When you are planning to domesticate mini lop rabbits, you should understand the licensing laws properly. This will help you to avoid future hassles with the law.

You should understand each detail before you go and buy the mini lop rabbit. In case you domesticate an animal against the law, the penalty could even include seizure of the animal.

It is important that you understand that the steps of obtaining the license would essentially be the same in most places, there could be slight variations between the various regions.

Different regions would have their own regulation set. This makes it essential for you to contact the local council of your region. Different regions have will have their own rules.

Licensing in United States

If you live in the United States of America, then you should know that there is no federal law governing the domestication of the mini lop rabbit. This means that you don't need a license in the United States of America.

Though there is no law that will prohibit you from keeping these rabbits, there are certain state laws that govern the keeping and also breeding of these animals. It is important to understand these state laws, so that you don't violate them.

It should be noted that certain areas require you to have a permit or license. Minnesota requires a person to acquire a permit at $15/£11.37 per year if he/she wishes to domesticate a mini lop rabbit. If the mini lop rabbit is not spayed or neutered, you can expect to pay even more.

A retail pet store owner does not require a permit or license to keep mini lop rabbits. It should also be noted that private rabbit collectors also don't need a license. But, if they plan to breed the rabbits, the laws will vary.

There are certain people who collect and breed these bunnies for exhibitions or wholesale benefits. If you belong to this category, then you might have to obtain a permit or license from the state. It is better to understand the rules and regulations of the local state council. This will help you to understand the laws that govern the keeping of mini lop rabbits in your particular area.

If you don't abide by the laws set by the central and state government, you will have to pay hefty fines as compensation. To avoid putting yourself in such a scenario, you should talk to rabbit owners in your area to understand the laws and should also visit the local council before you buy a mini lop bunny.

Licensing in United Kingdom

If you reside in the United Kingdom, then you should know that there is no legal law that governs the keeping of mini lop rabbits. Even breeders don't need a license or permit.

There are certain people who collect and breed these bunnies for exhibitions or wholesale benefits. If you belong to this category, even then you don't have to obtain a permit or license.

Though keeping of the mini lops is easy, the import and export of mini lop bunnies will require a permit. There is a license called AML, the Animal Movement License, which is required by a person trying to import or export a bunny from the United Kingdom.

Licensing outside United States and United Kingdom

If you reside outside the United States of America and the United Kingdom, even then you can domesticate a mini lop rabbit. It is important that you understand the regulations in your country.

It should be noted that there are many countries that allow the keeping and breeding of bunnies without the need of a permit and license. On the other hand, there are a few countries that require you to get a one time license or permit for keeping the bunny. In some countries, you might also have to pay a yearly fee to keep the rabbit.

Different countries have different laws for breeding of the animal. You should make sure that the laws are followed. If you fail to understand and follow the rules in your state, you might have to pay a hefty amount as a penalty.

To save yourself from any unpleasant happenings, you should learn the laws before you decide to buy the rabbit. Also, learn about the import and export laws if you are planning to import your bunny from somewhere else.

In extreme cases, the authorities might also take away your pet if you fail to abide by the laws. You should make sure that you don't have to face such issues. Do all that is required to domesticate the mini lop rabbit according to the set rules and regulations.

9. Bringing home a healthy pet

Many a times, people get so excited about buying the animal that they forget to do the basic checks that need to be done before bringing the animal to their house. You should definitely do all the checks before you buy the mini lop rabbit to avoid any future hassle.

There are many challenges that you will face while raising an animal at home. Your pet might face health issues that you would have to take care of. But, the last thing you want to do is to bring an unhealthy animal home.

It is always advised to discuss the health and also the history of the animal with the breeder before you buy the animal. A good breeder will not hesitate in sharing all the details about the animal with you.

You should make sure that you understand the various health issues that your future pet has suffered. If you are buying a mini lop rabbit that is older then it is all the more important to make sure that you understand the history of the animal. Discuss the various issues of the animal.

There are a few checks that you can conduct before you buy the mini lop rabbit. The following checks will help you to make sure that your rabbit is in good health and condition:

- To begin with, check the coat of the animal. You should look for any abrasions on the mini lop rabbit's skin. His skin should not be bruised anywhere.

- You should closely look for any injuries on the mini lop rabbit. If you find a mark or injury, make sure that you understand the cause of it. If it is a temporary issue, then it is fine. Discuss it with the breeder to make sure that the mark is not the indication of a serious issue with the mini lop rabbit's health.

- The fur of the mini lop rabbit is the indication of its health. If the fur is soft and shiny, you can be sure that the animal is healthy. On the other hand, if the fur is not good, then the pet has health issues for sure.

- Another simple check that you can perform on your rabbit is to check the body temperature of the mini lop rabbit. The body temperature should neither be too high nor too low. Make sure you discuss the right temperature range of the rabbit with your breeder.

- You should look for any hanging limbs in the animal. This is a clear indication of something being wrong with the animal. A hanging part of the body could mean that the pet is severely injured.

- You should also check the animal's eyes. The eyes should not be dull; they should be bright and shiny. This can also be an indication to the animal's current health.

10. Mini lop rabbits and other pets

If you are keen on domesticating mini lop rabbits with other pet animals, then it is important that you understand the temperament of the various animals.

Number of mini lop rabbits you can keep

If you are planning on keeping more than one mini lop rabbit, you should understand their behavioral and spatial requirements. If you already have a rabbit and are planning to buy more, you need to make sure that the pets can live together happily.

One of the most important criteria that need to be kept in mind is the space that you would provide the rabbits. The animals need the right amount of space to grow and develop.

These animals are known to be very active. You should be able to provide them a space where they can hop around without any constraints. There should be enough space for all the pets. If an animal has to compete with other animals for space, it will only lead to more trouble in the future.

The rabbits can get territorial and can fight with each other to establish their territory. You will have to keep a check on the pets to understand their basic behavior and their urge to establish a territory.

The rabbits can also grow fond of each other and live peacefully. Things will basically come down to the individual temperaments of the animals. You will have to devote some time to understanding it.

The age of the rabbits is another factor that should be taken into account. It is also known that if the rabbits are introduced to each other at a very young age, there is a chance that they will get along well.

It should be noted that you can keep a mini lop rabbit with other breeds of rabbits also, as long as there is space for everybody. An ideal scenario would be where you keep two to three rabbits. Remember to buy them at a young age so that they can grow together and bond well.

If you are looking to domesticate more than one mini lop rabbit, it is advised that you keep pairs of brothers and sisters. They will get along well. You can also keep pairs of males and females. As a rule, there should not be more than one male rabbit for two female rabbits.

Mini lop rabbits and other pets

Mini lop rabbits are social and loveable animals. You can expect your mini lop rabbit to be friendly towards other pets, but you will have to make sure that the pets are comfortable with each other.

If your mini lop rabbit is very young, you should make sure that you save him from bigger animals in the house that have a high prey drive. For example, a big cat might try to hunt the poor rabbit.

These animals might try to hurt the rabbit, and he would be too young to protect himself from any danger coming his way.

The type of pet is a very important criterion while determining whether the pets will get along or not. The mini lop rabbit will definitely get along with another sociable and friendly pet. If it finds the other animal a threat, then they will not get along.

If you are very keen on keeping more than one kind of pet in the household, then it is better that the mini lop rabbit and the other pets are made to socialize right from a young age. This will help them to bond well with each other.

The lesser the space for the animals, the more difficult it will get for you to raise your pets. So, space is one factor that will always be important when you are hand raising your pets. You should always keep this in mind.

No matter how things are looking, you should always keep a close eye on your pets. Never commit the mistake of leaving them on their own. You might not realize but they can harm each other. The first few interactions need to be all the more monitored.

If you notice your pets are not getting along well with each other, it is important that you don't force them to interact. They should be allowed to interact and bond in a very natural way. In the case where the pets can't get along even after multiple tries, you should keep them away from each other so that no one is harmed in any way.

Chapter 3: Meeting the nutritional needs of the mini lop rabbit

Diet and habitat are the two most important requirements of any pet. You have to make sure that the pet gets a good diet and an appropriate habitat.

This chapter and the following chapter will help you to understand the dietary requirements and the habitat requirements of your pet animal.

1. Why is diet consideration so important?

Diet is the most important factor that contributes to the growth of an animal. If your mini lop rabbit is well fed, you will see the positive effects on his health, his mood and his general behavior. So, taking care of your pet's diet should be a priority for you.

The rabbit would naturally be inclined to eating grass and some kinds of shrubs, but you can slowly introduce new food types for your hand-raised pet. You can introduce him to various other kinds of foods. You also need to make sure that enough water is given to the animal.

If you take care of the dietary requirements of the mini lop rabbit, you automatically take care of many other aspects. If your pet is eating tasty and nutritious food, he should be healthy, disease free, stress free and happy.

So, it is important that you make all the efforts to make sure that the pet is getting his daily dose of nutrition. This is your responsibility as the owner of the pet.

Another important point when deciding and finally buying the various food types for your pet is that a pet is totally dependent on you for its needs. It won't be able to tell you that the food is good or bad in quality.

As a parent, it is your duty to make sure that the food is of the highest quality. You should avoid buying any low quality food just to save some money.

You will have to be very careful when you are planning the diet for your pet. A good diet will help to keep the pet animal healthy and will also protect him from various diseases.

First and foremost, you should always keep the surroundings of the mini lop rabbit clean and tidy. Your bunny will try to eat anything and everything around it. This will have a hazardous effect on his health.

You might find your pet eating the sofa covers or little toys. You should make sure that small toys and other toxic items are not kept around the animal. The health of the pet is your responsibility.

2. Nutritional needs of the mini lop rabbit

The mini lop rabbit needs a diet that is rich in protein and fiber. The rabbits need high amounts of protein to supplement the growth of wool. You can see a decrease in the quantity and quality of the wool in a mini lop rabbit that is not fed high amounts of protein and fiber.

Fiber is also good for the general digestion of the animal. Sometimes, the rabbit can swallow some hair by mistake. The fiber in the diet of the pet will help him to avoid any harmful consequences because of swallowing of the hair.

The food habits of captive bunnies vary slightly from wild bunnies. As the owner of the pet, you have to make sure that the pet gets to eat what he ate in his natural habitat. Along with that, other foods should also be introduced to him.

It should be noted that the main components of the diet of the mini lop rabbit should be fresh vegetables, pellets and hay. It is important that the food that is served to the rabbit helps him to stay healthy. He should not gain much weight from it.

If the rabbit eats too much food, he can gain weight, which is a hindrance to his normal body functions. You should regulate the food that you serve the rabbit. On a daily basis, you can give him half a cup of pellets and one full cup of organic fresh vegetables.

It is always suggested that the quality of food is maintained. It is better to serve fresh and organic vegetables. This will ensure good health for the bunny. You can serve good amounts of hay to the rabbit. Hay will not make the rabbit fat. Let him eat as much as he wants to.

Hay

Hay should be the main component of the mini lop rabbit's diet. It is important that he is allowed to eat as much hay as he wants to, as hay has many benefits for the rabbit. It is not possible to give the rabbit optimal nutrition by avoiding hay.

If the rabbit is eating good quantities of hay, he can save himself from intestinal blockages. Intestinal blockages can be very dangerous for the health of the rabbit. The issue of hairballs can also be controlled if the rabbit is eating good quantities of hay.

You should avoid Lucerne hay for the rabbit. It can cause diarrhoea in the rabbit if it is served in huge quantities.

Pellets

Pellets should also be served to the mini lop rabbit in the right quantities. You can serve half a cup to the rabbit every day.

If you are one of those people who buy pellets in bulk, then you should know the right way to store them. You should make sure that the pellets are safely stored in an airtight container because moisture can spoil the pellets.

If the pellets catch moisture, they will go mouldy. These kinds of pellets are not good for the mini lop because they can lead to diseases.

You will find a guinea pig and rabbit mix in most stores. This is a mix of dried fruits, seeds, nuts and corn. Do not serve this to the mini lop. This kind of a mix is not required by the bunny. It can make the mini lop gain weight because of the high fat in the mix.

Pellets can be given to both the young and the adult rabbits. But, if you are not keen on serving the rabbits pellets, then make sure that at least the young rabbit is served these pellets. You can discontinue the use after the bunny matures.

A young rabbit should not be deprived of any nutrients, as this is the growing stage, and you need to be cautious.

It should be noted here that if you wish to discontinue the use of pellets for the adult bunny, then you have to make sure that the mini lop rabbit is getting all the nutrition from the food it is eating. You should serve him good quality hay, vegetables and fruits to ensure that he is eating the right kinds of foods.

Fresh vegetables and fruits

It is advised to serve vegetables after the rabbit is three to four months of age. A mini lop rabbit loves to eat sweets. The fruits that you should serve him will do for the sweet requirement of the bunny.

You can serve the bunny a piece of apple, a few grapes or one sultana at a time. You should make sure that you don't overdo it. If you serve large quantities of fruits to the rabbit, he might not be able to digest the same.

Vegetables are also essential for the rabbit. You should make sure that you serve only high quality vegetables to the mini lop rabbit. Don't give him stale or spoilt vegetables because this will have a negative effect on his health.

You should look at serving him only organic vegetables and fruits. You can also grow your own vegetables if you have the space and time. The rule should be that if the vegetable or fruit is not fit for your consumption, it is not fit for the bunny's consumption.

Water

A mini lop rabbit needs good amounts of water for its survival. You should make sure that the animal always has access to drinking water.

Water helps the mini lop rabbit regulate its body temperature. The rabbit has a coat of fur over his body, and it is very important that the body of the pet maintains the right temperature.

If the mini lop rabbit is not hydrated well, he can develop severe health complications. You can even lose your pet mini lop rabbit because of a lack of water in his system. To avoid such things, make sure that the pet is hydrated at all times.

If you keep a water container in the hutch or cage of the pet mini lop rabbit, there is a high probability that the pet will play in the water. Even if he does not play, the water can spill easily in the cage or over the mini lop rabbit.

The water can wet the coat of the mini lop rabbit and it is important that the wool of the rabbit is always dry. Wet wool is the source of many health issues, especially skin-related diseases in the pet animal.

You should buy chew-proof water bottles for the mini lop rabbits. These bottles can be easily placed in the hutch or cage of the rabbit and are easily available.

It is easy to clean these water bottles. There are special brushes available in pet stores and also online that will allow you to clean the water bottles easily and without a fuss. Make sure that you clean them at least once a week.

You should also make sure that you purchase the right extensions to attach to the water bottle. These extensions will allow you to keep the water bottles in place and will also allow you to fix them at the right angle in the cage of the pet bunny.

If you live in a place where water freezes during winters, you will have to take special care of the mini lop rabbit. You might be busy at work and all the water in the water bottle could be frozen.

Such a condition can force the pet to go without water for extended periods, which is extremely dangerous for the mini lop rabbit. A simple solution to this problem is to use heated bowls in winter, but with this the same issue of the coat getting wet arises. To make things simpler, you need to check at regular intervals that the water is not frozen.

3. Foods to avoid

You should make it a rule never to feed anything to the mini lop rabbit, unless you are sure that it is good for the rabbit. In many cases, people feed them certain foods assuming that if humans can consume them, then rabbits can.

However, this is not true. There are many food types that are good for humans and many other animals but not suitable for your mini lop rabbit. You will jeopardize the health of the pet if you are not careful about what you serve to him.

Sometimes, the children of the house can force the pet animal to consume toxic and unhealthy food items just for fun. This can prove to be fatal for the rabbit.

It is important that you keep a check on what the kids are doing with the pet animal. It is always advised to let the children interact with the rabbit under an adult's supervision.

Keep the food of the rabbit fresh, simple and healthy. When you are giving fruit, you should make sure that it does not have seeds because the seeds can be poisonous for the pet rabbit.

If you are looking for a comprehensive list of food items that are unhealthy for the rabbit, then the given list will help you. You should avoid these food items:

- Caffeine

- Bread

- Citrus peels

- Corn

- Fresh peas

- Grains

- Green beans and legumes

- Rice

- Nuts

- Rhubarb leaves

- Seeds

- Sugar

- Beets

- Chocolates and cocoa beans

- Onion and potatoes

- Avocado

- Cookies, cakes and candy.

You can also contact 'Pet poison control' authority in severe cases.

4. Treats

Treats are an essential part of a pet's meal plan. Treats are like small meal gifts that make the pet happy and delighted. The anticipation of getting a treat can also keep his behavior in check.

You should work on giving your pet high quality treats. The treat should be tasty but also nutritious. The mini lop rabbit should look forward to receiving a treat from you. This section will give you an idea of the kind of treats you can include in your rabbit's meal plan.

It should be noted that just because your mini lop rabbit seems to enjoy a treat, you can't give the food item to him all day long. You will have to keep a check on the amount of treats a pet will get. This is important because treats are not food replacements, they are only small rewards.

It is also important that the pet associates the treat with a reward. He should know that he is being served the treat reward for a reason. You should also make sure that the treats are healthy for the pet.

If you keep serving him the wrong kinds of treats, it will only affect his health in the long run. This is the last thing that you would want as a parent of the pet.

The treat should have the right mix of vitamins, fatty acids, minerals and proteins. This will make the treat healthy and wholesome. It is better if the treat has no sugar content. This is because the sugar will add no food value to the treat. Such healthy treats can be given to the pet on a daily basis without any issues.

Be careful if you are planning to give your pet a bowl of nuts or fruits as a treat. If you think that all fruits can serve as a treat for the pet, then you are absolutely wrong. Though a small amount of certain fruits should be fine, a larger quantity will affect the health of the pet. You should avoid nuts because they are toxic for the mini lop rabbit.

The pet can suffer from diarrhea and other gastro intestinal problems because of consuming large amount of toxic food. You will be shocked to know the problems that an undigested vegetable or fruit can cause in a mini lop rabbit.

If there is a piece of undigested food in the digestive tract of the animal, it can lead to obstructions and blockages. This will lead to many other digestive tract-related complications.

The bowel movements of the pet can be restricted or completely stopped because of the undigested food. This can even pose a very serious threat to the life of the animal.

You should also make sure that you peel and mash the items before you serve them to the animal. This will allow him to digest the food well. There have been many reports of blockages in rabbits because of undigested peels and seeds.

5. How much should you feed the mini lop rabbit?

As a new owner or a prospective owner, this is another concern that you must be having. It is recommended that you keep a bowl of food available for the pet at all times. If your pet is not well and the vet has advised you to feed him less, then you can alter the quantities of food items that you serve him.

There are many owners who decrease the quantity of food they feed the pet animal if he happens to gain some weight. You are advised not to do so. This can be detrimental for the health of the pet.

If your mini lop rabbit has gained some weight, you should focus on increasing the amount of activity that he gets. Don't deprive him of his food. This will have a negative effect on the health of the mini lop rabbit.

Good exercise and food high in protein and fiber are enough for the mini lop rabbit to lose weight and remain healthy. You can also expect a relatively younger mini lop rabbit to eat more than the adults.

It is said that one of the first signs of health issues in a mini lop rabbit is a change in his appetite. You should always keep an eye on whether the pet is eating well or not.

A simple way to keep track of the mini lop rabbit's diet is to check his food bowl after every meal he has. If you see any abrupt change in his food habits, you should consult the doctor. It is always better to catch a health problem in the earliest stages.

6. Introducing new foods to the mini lop rabbits

If you want to introduce new foods or switch foods, you can't suddenly change the rabbit's usual meal plan. This will put the bunny off. He might even give up eating altogether. This is something that you would never want.

The mini lop rabbit will naturally be inclined to eat hay and grass. You should also introduce him to certain vegetables and fruit. This will have a very positive effect on his overall health.

It is suggested that the pet should be introduced to different food types quite early in his life. This will make it easier for you and also for the pet mini lop rabbit. This will help the bunny to have his preferences and will also make things easier for you.

If you don't introduce new foods to the pet mini lop rabbit, he will turn out to be a very fussy eater. In addition, you will find it very difficult to provide him with the right types of food.

You should slowly introduce new foods to the pet. There are some simple tips and tricks that you should be following to make sure that the pet is eating well even when new foods are being introduced.

You should introduce one new food at a time. A simple way of introducing new food in the diet of the mini lop rabbit is by starting out with a small amount of the food. Take a bowl and add the usual food of the pet in it. Now, take a very small amount of the new food that you wish to feed your pet in the bowl. Mix the contents and serve the food to the pet animal.

You should remember that the rabbit needs time to get used to it. There is nothing to worry about even if the pet leaves the new food in the beginning. Just keep adding a very small amount of the food item to the usual food of the pet. This might take some time so be prepared. Once you see that the pet has started eating the new food along with the usual old food, you can gradually increase the portion of the new food.

7. Food for a young mini lop bunny

You have to be a little more careful when you are planning the menu for your young mini lop bunny. If a growing rabbit is not given the right nutrients in the right quantity then the rabbit can develop some serious health issues, which can get bigger with time.

If your mini lop rabbit is under the age of four months, then you can serve him as much food as he can eat. Observe the amount of food he eats for a few days then accordingly serve him his daily dose of food.

You should give more quantities of hay than any other food items. If your young bunny is under three months then make sure that you don't serve him large amounts of fruits and vegetables. It is better to serve him hay and pellets.

It is better to start vegetables and fruits only after the rabbit is three months of age. You should never serve him large amounts suddenly. It is always better to slowly introduce the vegetables and fruits.

You should increase the amount slowly. Take a week or so to introduce the bunny to vegetables and fruits. Every second or third day, give him a few pieces. Alter the amount of vegetables and fruits that you serve him.

During this time, keep a close eye on him. Is the bunny able to digest the food? Is the bunny rejecting the food? Is he uncomfortable? Is he suffering from diarrhoea? Does he like the new foods?

These questions will help you to give the right food to your young bunny. A little experiment from your side will also help the bunny to get used to the new food. Within two to three months, the young mini lop will start eating and enjoying the vegetables and fruits that you serve him.

Chapter 4: Habitat requirements

If you can't provide your pet a habitat that keeps him happy and safe, then you will fail as the owner of the pet. You need to make sure that the pet gets what would make it happy and comfortable. The animal can slip into sadness and depression if his habitat requirements are not met.

Pets require proper shelter so that you can keep them safe from the changes in weather and also from possible attacks from predators. It is advisable that you make the necessary arrangements for your pet before you bring him home so that you can get them straight into their shelter when they are home.

1. Building a good shelter

Proper shelters are extremely important for your pet. When the weather is not suitable, or if the pet is unwell or if the animal wants to simply rest, having good housing is a must.

Construction

The construction should ensure that there are no projections on the surface of the cage or shelter to prevent injury. You must clean all the exposed surfaces and disinfect them to ensure the good health of your pet.

If you are using treated wood or any paint on the surface of the construction material, it should not be toxic to the mini lop rabbit.

Wooden material requires preservatives to prevent any chance of rotting or warping. The flooring should be leveled as much as possible and must not be slippery. Good drainage is necessary to make sure that any waste is drained out.

The doors should be wide enough for the mini lop rabbit. The height should be such that the rabbit does not hurt himself while playing. Use bolts on the top and bottom to make sure that the door is fastened well when the mini lop rabbit is inside.

You can even have a top door that can be secured when in the open position. The disadvantage with a top door is that ventilation and sunlight is reduced when it is closed.

The shelter should also have good lighting to ensure that the mini lop rabbit can see properly. The keeper should be able to examine the animal and handle it safely.

You can have portable lighting as well. If you do plan to install the lighting inside the shelter, make sure that the bulbs are out of the rabbit's reach. The cabling should be secure and of high quality to prevent any chance of fires or short circuits.

The air circulation should be adequate while ensuring that there are no drafts inside the shelter. You can even install safety glass with each window to keep the shelter warm. It is best to keep one window open at all times unless the temperature drops drastically.

If you do not provide enough ventilation, there are chances that your mini lop rabbit will develop respiratory issues. While airflow should be kept at a maximum, you need to keep a constant check on the dust that is entering the shelter.

Ideally, the size of the shelter should be large enough to allow the rabbit to rise easily, turn around while inside the shelter and also maintain a safe distance from the other rabbits that you may have housed inside the shelter. If you have a large space that houses many pets, space for each pet should be the top priority.

Safety

A shelter should be able to keep the pet animal safe. He should be safe from predators and also from hazards such as fire. You will have to take into consideration all the fire safety recommendations that are laid out by your local government.

If you are unsure, you can also seek advice from a Fire Prevention Officer in your locality to understand the statutory requirements. If you have any combustible liquid or material in the area surrounding the shelter, it should be removed instantly. You should also make sure that you do not smoke in the shelter area or in the areas near it.

Fire extinguishers, alarm systems and other equipment should be checked on a regular basis by someone who is qualified. If you have any electrical installation in the shelter, it should be periodically inspected and maintained. The fittings and wires should not be accessible to the pets.

You must also make sure that it is earthed properly and is kept safe from any rodents. If you need to use extension cables and leads, you should make sure that it does not get entangled in the legs of the animal, leading to serious injuries.

Metal pipe work and any steel that is used in the structure should be earthed well. You can take additional precautions by ensuring that all the installations are protected by an RCD; a residual current device.

Lastly, in case there is an outbreak of a fire, you should make sure that your pet animal or animals can be released easily. A fire exit should be installed and an emergency turnout procedure should be planned and communicated to everyone who is working with the pets. This is necessary when you are housing a large number of pets in a designated area.

2. Types of shelters

The habitat should be spacious, comfortable and safe for the pet. The pet should feel at home in the habitat that you provide it. You should try to furnish the enclosure in a way that the cage resembles the natural habitat of the rabbit. This will keep him happy and upbeat, which is essential for his overall well being.

If you are looking for shelter ideas for your pet mini lop rabbit, then you would be happy to know that you have many options. This section will explore the various shelter ideas for a mini lop rabbit.

The pet is more like a new member of the family, a new baby in the house. So when you buy the animal, you should make sure that you understand the needs of the animal at various stages of his life. It is better to spend some extra money in the beginning than to see your pet being sad and lonely in the shelter. You should make sure that you understand this before you finalize a cage for the pet.

Building the ideal cage

You can buy or build a cage for your pet rabbit. It is very important to design and build the right enclosure for the rabbit. The enclosure will be like a home to the rabbit, so it is very important that the enclosure meets all the requirements of the rabbit.

A good amount of enclosure space is essential when designing and planning the cage. This is because the pet rabbit needs some space to move around. The cage should not feel like a prison. It has to be safe and secure.

The ideal cage of the rabbit should be 6 x 2 x 2 feet. These dimensions of the enclosure are the minimum requirements of the mini lop rabbit. It is advised to keep the size six times the size of the mini lop rabbit.

There might be an instance when you would have to isolate your mini lop rabbit. Your habitat should allow you to do so. The isolation could be needed due to some disease or infection that the animal could be suffering from.

The isolated area would help the animal to be treated well. This will also help in keeping the other pets in the house safe.

A simple trick that you can use to make the animal comfortable with the cage is to instruct the bunny to go inside the cage, but leave the door of the cage open. If you do this, the mini lop rabbit will also not feel captive.

Let the rabbit come out and go inside the cage at will, but make sure that it spends considerable time in the cage. It is important that the pet is not forced to go into the cage. He should find the cage homely and should go there without a hesitation.

If you are unable to supervise the pet for some reason, don't make the mistake of keeping the cage door open. You should keep the cage door closed so that the pet stays inside. This is to avoid any unpleasant incidents.

You should always remember that no matter how much you train the rabbit, you can be surprised and shocked by him. He is a playful, chirpy and active animal and will not miss any chance to make some mischief.

It is extremely important that you clean the cage regularly. A dirty cage will only lead to infections for the pet and also other pets. You should clean the cage daily and should change the food and water provided for him.

The outdoor enclosure should be planned and constructed keeping in mind the basic nature of the rabbit. The animal should have fun, but should also be safe and should not get any opportunity to run away from the enclosure.

The enclosure needs to be constructed with high quality material. The outer area of your garden and backyard should also be covered. You can look at using the chain links that are utilized to build cyclone fences. These fences are very strong and durable.

There is a chance that while playing, the rabbit's head might just get stuck in a gap in the fence. To prevent any such accident, you can install a preventive wire outside the main fence. This will ensure that the rabbit does not get trapped when you are not around.

You have to take preventive measures so that the mini lop rabbit does not climb out. You should make sure that the enclosure has fencing on the top area. The rabbit also loves digging. It should also be taken care of that the rabbit can't dig and eventually escape the enclosure.

The enclosure should be safe and also well fenced. This will make sure that the rabbit can't escape. To make things look like his natural habitat, cover the floor with sand, plants, wooden chips and twigs. Your house should have fencing to protect the pet animal from stray animals. The pet should be able to be at peace when in the enclosure. He should be able to do whatever he wants.

Rabbit hutch

A rabbit hutch can be defined as a cage for the rabbit that is constructed generally with wood and a wire mesh that surrounds it. Most rabbit hutches have long legs to keep them anywhere. The ones without legs can be placed over tables or other safe surfaces.

Building a rabbit hutch is one of the most popular choices. You should make sure that you have the provisions to build it in your house. You can keep one in the backyard, basement or any other area of the house.

It is important that you understand that a rabbit hutch is only one option that you have when your pet needs to be kept in a cage-like environment. This does not mean that you keep the pet in the hutch and forget about him.

The hutch needs to be easily accessible to you or a family member. You should check on the rabbit from time to time. You should also allow the pet some time outside the hutch to just walk around.

Many cases have been reported in the past where the owners' negligence towards the mini lop rabbits caused serious issues in the animals, such as stress and depression. You can't abandon your rabbit in a comfortable hutch. The pet should be kept indoors as much as possible. The hutch can be used when you are not around to care for the pet.

You can buy the rabbit hutch or can design it yourself. It is important that it meets all the requirements of the pet animal. To begin with, the hutch needs to be spacious. The animal should have enough space to walk around.

You should make sure that the rabbit hutch does not suffocate the rabbit. It should be airy and well ventilated. You should make sure that the rabbit has access to food and water in the rabbit hutch. You can install a feed hopper and a good watering system in the rabbit hutch to ensure the same.

You should also try to make the hutch attractive for the rabbit. He should not feel bored and suffocated in there. The hutch should feel like a fun home for him. There are some simple ways in which you can make the hutch a lively place for the rabbit.

Keep some small and interesting toys for the Mini lop rabbit in the hutch. You should make sure that the toys don't scare the pet away. They should be inviting and fun for him. This will keep him happy and entertained.

The rabbit hutch should allow proper sanitation. Many cases of diseases have been reported in mini lop rabbits due to improper sanitation.

The rabbit's hutch would need to be cleaned regularly to make sure that there are no disease carrying bacteria and viruses in there. These are simple things, but critical when it comes to the well being of the pet in the long run.

The nest boxes that are used for the kits should be sanitized regularly. They should be stored safely and properly when not in use. You can store them and use them for the next set of kits that you might have.

If you are planning to keep more than one mini lop rabbit, then you can work on giving them a common habitat. Some people would choose to give separate shelters to the animals. The idea of providing separate shelters is also fine.

If the pets get along, then they can be kept in a common cage. However, in case the rabbits are not getting along, keeping them in a common cage will only lead to more problems in the future, so this should be avoided.

If you are planning on domesticating more than one rabbit, you can consider buying another cage. This cage could be very simple and basic. The main purpose of this extra cage is to use it when one of the rabbits is sick. The cage will help you to isolate the sick pet animal.

A vet will always advise you to isolate a sick pet. This is necessary so that the pet can recover nicely in the absence of other pets. He would need some space to himself. What is also important is that he should not transmit the disease to the healthy pets. The isolation helps to avoid such a situation.

Precautions with outdoor hutch

If you are planning to keep an outdoor hutch, there are a few precautions that you would have you would have to take. These simple steps and precautions will ensure that the pet bunny is happy and safe in outdoor enclosure.

Firstly, the outdoor hutch needs to be kept in a shady area. If the place gets too hot for the rabbit, it can lead to stress in the animal. This is especially important in summers and if you live in a place that is mostly hot.

The outdoor enclosure needs to be kept in a way that you can be sure that all predators are away from the hutch. You could be busy inside the house while some predator might attack and even kill the poor mini lop rabbit.

The mini lop rabbit is very small in size. This makes it easy prey for some ferocious animals such as the fox, dog and cat. It is important to take the right measures to save the mini lop rabbit from these dangerous and ferocious predators.

3. Accessories

When you bring a pet home, the pet will be scared of the new surroundings. You will have to make all the attempts that will help the pet to adjust in the new environment.

When you are planning the furnishing and accessories of the shelter, you should make sure that you give the pet an environment that closely resembles his natural habitat. This will keep him happy and spirited.

Besides the basic stuff such as food and water, it is also important to accessorize the cage well. This is important because the right accessories will help him to feel like he is at home. They will bring him closer to his natural habitat and natural tendencies.

There are several accessories available these days that will help you to keep your pet happy. If you go to a pet toyshop, you will get many ideas for the accessories that you can keep in the cage of the pet.

Bedding

Keeping your pets warm is very important. For this, adequate bedding material is necessary. This not only provides warmth but also protects the animal against any chance of injury. When the mini lop rabbit lies down on the floor, he will be comfortable with good bedding.

The bedding material should be free from mold and too much dust. The material should also be non-toxic to a mini lop rabbit. The best option is matting, as it is also absorbent by nature.

You can even add material like straw, shavings and other material that can absorb any urine. This should be changed regularly and well managed to ensure complete hygiene and disease prevention.

There are many types of bedding available these days that can help your pet to have rest and fun when he wants. For example, you can get bedding in the shape of a cave. This will be fun for the pet. The right kind of bedding provided for the rabbit is a simple way of keeping the pet animal comfortable and stress-free.

There are cage liners easily available on the market. You can use these to line the bottom of the cage. They are easy to attach and detach, so are very popular amongst owners.

It is also important that the cage is deep for this type of setting. The liners should be made from a good quality fabric. These liners are safe for the pet because they don't have sharp pieces that can hurt him.

It is easier for the pet to walk on these liners. Fabric liners are actually considered the best option for a bunny's cage. One disadvantage of these liners would be that the pet will try to dig into them and might also spill his food and water. It can be inconvenient to the pet-parent at such a time.

Another popular choice of bedding for the cage is wood shavings. It is important that the shavings are free from phenol. It is also important that the cage is deep; otherwise the shavings will just fall off.

The pet can safely dig in these wood shavings. He can have his fun in this simple way. The wood shavings are relatively odorless because they allow air amongst the shavings.

The wood shavings also have some disadvantages. The shavings will keep falling in the eyes of the pet or they might fall in the water or food containers.

You can use aspen shavings. They are considered the safest of all. The second choice of shavings could be kiln dried pine shavings. You should not use untreated pine shavings or cedar shavings. These can be harmful for the pet.

If you can't install liners in the cage of the mini lop rabbit, then paper shavings is your second best option. They look quite similar to wood shavings.

One downside of this kind of bedding is that the paper bedding is very dusty in nature. This might lead to dry skin in your mini lop rabbit. If your pet already has dry skin, the condition might be aggravated.

Rugs and blankets

You can also keep a couple of warm blankets inside the cage. The bunny will play and will also bite them. The rabbit will also like snuggling into the blanket. You should try to make the cage as comfortable as possible, so that the pet animal does not feel like captive and starts liking the cage.

If the mini lop rabbit is old, clipped or is injured, you have to keep him protected from any draft or low temperature. You can also use these rugs to keep flies at bay. Any turnout rug should be removed in case the weather improves to prevent the cage from getting very warm.

The size of the rug should be big enough to suit the size of the bunny. You need the right size to ensure that there are no abrasions, hair loss or restricted movements. They should be removed on a regular basis to check the body condition of the pet. You should also make sure that the bunny does not get too hot because of the rug being on him constantly.

The rugs should be cleaned and repaired regularly. In case of any wetness in the rugs, you should have a spare one that you can use on your pet animal. These precautions ensure that the animal stays clear of any illnesses.

Containers for food and water

It is also extremely important that you give due importance to the containers that would be used to serve food and water to the mini lop rabbits. What makes this important is the fact that dirty containers are carriers of allergies and diseases. These allergies and diseases can further turn into serious issues if not treated well.

The containers should also be sturdy enough to hold all the food and water. They should also allow the pet to feed himself without any difficulty. So, even if you have not thought of selecting containers as an important step in animal care, you can do so now.

The food containers should be of good quality and should ideally be made of aluminum or good grade plastic. A poor quality container will only contribute towards spoiling the food, which is something you will never want. The spoilt food is not just a hassle for you, but is also harmful to the health of your bunny.

A water container has some limitations. It can lead to a wet coat for the rabbit, which in turn can lead to many water borne diseases. You can use specialized water bottles to keep water for the rabbit in the cage.

If you are concerned about the soiling of the food or if you have more than one pet that would eat from the same food container, then a hayrack could be your ideal buy. A trough or pellet bin with hayracks will help you to avoid the soiling of food items.

The container would also allow more than one animal to eat from the same container. You should choose a size that is most ideal for you. Each animal should get enough space to eat comfortably.

The containers should be washed with good quality soap powder at least twice a week. It is very important that the containers are kept clean at all times. Do not forget to remove the leftover food or dirty water from the containers.

There are many different kinds of feeders available today. You should go for a feeder that suits your needs the best.

Toys

You also have to make sure that the pet is entertained. The pet can get bored easily, which will make him a little aggressive. To keep him occupied, you can keep various kinds of toys in the pet's cage.

The right kind of toys should be bought for the pets. You will get many ideas when you visit a shop that sells toys for rabbits, but it is important that the toys are of good quality. They should not be harmful for the pet.

It is better if the toys are washable. This will enable you to wash the pet's toys every now and then when they are dirty. The harmful bacteria will also be removed from the toys when they are washed.

In addition, make sure that the toys can't be shredded by the animal. If the pet is able to shred the toy, he will swallow the shreds. This is very harmful and will only invite more trouble for the pet. To avoid all these issues, buy the right kind of toys.

You should remember that the furnishing should also be designed keeping in mind the comfort and also the security of the pet. The furnishing should not in any way disturb the lifestyle of the rabbit. It should gel with the personality of the animal.

A simple way to keep the rabbit happy is to give him an old t-shirt or piece of cloth. The pet will love it. He will act as if he is digging in the t-shirt. He will also try to fit in the t-shirt. This will keep him busy and happy.

4. Cleaning the habitat

The pet can't clean the cage on its own, and if it is forced to stay in an unhygienic environment, he will fall sick. It is extremely important to clean the cage of the pet. You will not necessarily enjoy this process, but still you have to do it.

The first thing you need to make sure is that the housing area is properly sanitized. Building the housing area on an elevated area is one of the best measures to keep it from having any build-up of moisture.

There are certain tasks that you need to do daily, while several others need to be done once a week. Similarly, if the food and water containers look dirty, they should be cleaned and refilled. It is best that you clean out the feeding and water containers on a daily basis.

The food and water must be replaced to prevent the bunny from eating any rotten or spoiled food. It is important that the cage is free from all bacteria and viruses that are known to cause diseases in pet animals. You should keep some time designated for the cleaning of the cage.

At least once a week, the litter and the bedding material should be changed. In case you notice any dampness in the bedding, it needs to be changed immediately. Damp areas encourage the growth of fungi. They are the primary cause for respiratory issues and skin troubles in bunnies.

To clean the shelter thoroughly, you have to start by dusting and dry cleaning. You will have to sweep the floor of the coop and dust off the ceiling.

All the fixtures, nest boxes, air inlets and fans must be dusted. The feed from the feeders should be removed. Any feces and debris is scraped off the floor and the perches. You can even vacuum the floor as an option.

The power should be turned off before you wet clean the cage. There are some basic steps that you need to follow each time you clean the cage.

Any area that is heavily soiled can be soaked with a low-pressure sprayer. Until the manure and dirt is softened, keep it soaked so you can remove it easily.

All the surfaces in the shelter should be cleaned out fully. Focus on the ceiling trusses, the walls, the windowsills and any area where dust may accumulate. Use a mild detergent with pH that ranges between 6 and 8. A mild alkali solution like baking soda solution can be sprayed around to disinfect the shelter thoroughly.

Rinsing the soap off completely before you allow it to dry is a good idea. Use plain water to rinse and make sure that there aren't any puddles left behind in the shelter.

The shelter can be allowed to dry by air-drying the building. All the windows and vents should be opened. It is a good idea to use a fan or a blower if possible. The best option is to clean when the weather is warm and sunny. This improves the drying process.

Any repairs in the area should be made before you disinfect the shelter one final time. The rodent holes should be sealed, lighting fixtures must be repaired and any breakages or protruding areas in the construction must be repaired.

The most crucial step is the final disinfecting, which is usually overlooked by those who have a small hutch or cage. Once the whole shelter has been washed, rinsed and dried, you should use a good disinfectant.

Your veterinarian will be able to provide you with spray or fumigation options. The best option with most small shelters is to use a mild spray to disinfect it.

Make sure you follow the instructions provided by the manufacturer with respect to diluting the disinfectant. Usually you will need about one gallon of the diluted disinfectant per 200 square feet of space of the shelter.

Another point that you need to understand is that you should not use very strong disinfectants. Such products can be very harmful if they are ingested even in the smallest of quantities.

You should always look for mild anti bacterial soaps and detergents to clean the vessels and the floor.

If you want the process to be more thorough, you can even soak all the feeders and the bowls in 200-ppm chlorine solution. You can make that by mixing 1 tablespoon of chlorine bleach in a gallon of boiling water. With these steps, you should be able to raise a pet that is in the best of its health.

Chapter 5: Proofing the house

You should know that a pet left on his own has a tendency to injure himself. Your mini lop rabbit is a cute and small animal, but if proper precautions are not taken, it can create havoc in your home. It is very important that you learn the simple ways to bunny proof the home.

The worst nightmare of any prospective caregiver is when the pet animal creates a mess in the house. This can be very difficult for anyone that wishes to domesticate an animal.

Though bunnies are very calm by their natural demeanour, they are also very curious. They have the capacity to chew off things if they are not supervised from time to time.

When you have a pet at home, you have to ensure that the pet is safe at all times. This is one of your basic responsibilities as the pet owner. A rabbit has a very curious personality.

The mini lop rabbit will not think twice before charging into unknown territory. The animal is so small that he can easily get himself into problems. This makes it very important that you understand the behaviour of your pet very well.

This chapter is meant to help you to understand the various ways to bunny proof your home. Make sure you bunny proof your home and keep your pet bunny away from potential dangers.

You might be busy with work, and before you know your pet mini lop might be walking into some real danger. It is important to learn some basic ways to bunny proof the house.

When you take appropriate measures to bunny proof the house, you can actually go a long way in ensuring that the rabbit is safe and there are no unwanted incidents in the house.

It is always better to take precautions, rather than lamenting when a major damage has been done because in most cases, the damage can't be reserved or undone.

You should know that your pet bunny has a tendency to injure himself. If you don't pay attention, the damage could be very serious and irrevocable. A very simple solution to keep your pet animal safe is to bunny proof your home.

This chapter will discuss the potential dangers to the mini lop rabbits and also some simple ways to bunny proof your house. They will help you to avoid mishaps and also keep the mini lop rabbit safe at all times.

1. Why should you bunny proof your house?

Many of you might be wondering why it is so important to bunny proof the house. If you fail to bunny proof your house, you might find your pet seriously injuring himself.

It is important that you take appropriate steps to bunny proof the home. This will help you to set some limits and boundaries for the pet. These boundaries are for his own good.

There is no use in getting cautious after serious and irrevocable damage has been done. It pays to take all the necessary precautions right from the very beginning.

You will take some time to understand the mannerisms of your pet. It is important to always supervise the pet. But, once you understand the pet better, you can take steps to make sure that things remain safe in the house for the pet. A safe environment is good for everybody in the home.

If you are unable to do so, you can ask a family member to do so for you. You can use the cage when there is no one around to supervise the pet rabbit. You can be secure knowing that your pet is safe and sound inside its cage.

The rabbit can injure himself and can also lead to mishaps in the house. This can be very dangerous not just for the rabbit, but also for the family members.

You should be very serious about pet proofing your home. Your mini lop rabbit could just chew something dangerous and die. If your pet swallows something toxic, you might not even get a chance to take him to the veterinarian and save him.

This makes it very important to look for areas of hidden dangers and keep the pet safe. These animals have a tendency to chew everything they can.

It will chew your rugs and carpets. It will chew on rubber items, though such things are very harmful for him. It is you who needs to make sure that the pet does not chew on the wrong items.

It is also important to save your household things from the pet rabbit. You can't let him chew away your favourite carpet or coat. You will have to make sure that your stuff is safe and the pet is also safe.

It is also important to note that if the pet swallows something, blockages can happen easily and they can be very dangerous. There are many rabbits that lose their lives because of such blockages.

Mini lop rabbits are so fond of chewing that they will chew on anything. They will chew on rubber items and foam and sponge based products. While they might like chewing on them, these materials when ingested will cause blockage of the digestive tract.

The animal is also very fond of digging tunnels. He will try to dig a tunnel or burrow for itself wherever it can. If you don't pay attention, you might find your rabbit chewing and digging your favourite sofa.

You should understand that he is an animal and wouldn't know what is right or wrong for him. It is you who is responsible for your pet. You have to take measures to avoid such incidents in your home.

Your pet will love digging your sofa and couch. He will try to climb on the furniture and try to chew on the stuffing. He will also not miss an opportunity to chew on paper and plastic items.

These things are extremely dangerous for him if he swallows them. If you don't keep an eye on him, your bunny will chew away all your expensive sofas. This is the simple reason why it is expected that the pet is supervised at all times.

Mini lop rabbits are also attracted to plants. They will merrily chew on the leaves of various plants. Many house plants are known to be poisonous for the bunny, so they should not be encouraged to eat the leaves.

Additionally, they like digging and tunnelling. So, the animal would try to dig in the sofa material. You should be on the lookout of any tell-tale signs. If you see stuffing material on the floor, you should know what the mini lop has been up to. He should be stopped as soon as possible.

If he has been chewing on it, then you know that you will have to keep the bunny away from them. These things are very harmful for the pet. And, it is also very costly for you on the whole.

The animal has a tendency to walk in to a situation and then not know what to do next. He might just climb on to the top of a closet, not knowing what to do.

Rabbits will also crawl into any opening they see. For example, the pet might get under the small opening of a fridge or refrigerator. This is very dangerous because the fan of the fridge can harm him.

Similarly, washing machines and dish washers are potential dangers to the animal. The best way to keep your pet animal out of danger is to know where he is and what he is up to. This will mean that you can help him if he has landed himself into some kind of danger.

You need to be cautious when you are using store bought detergents and bleaching powder to clean surfaces and washrooms. If they have poisonous and toxic stuff, they can be harmful for the bunny.

To be on the safer side, you should always rinse the surfaces with excess water. This will make sure that the detergent has been washed off. Make sure that the pet does not have access to such harmful things.

There could be so many things in your house that look non-dangerous, but could be very dangerous for your rabbit. This is the reason that you might have to monitor the pet animal when he is not in his cage.

It is also a good idea to designate a spare room in the house for the mini lop rabbit. This room should be open and spacious. It should have natural light and good ventilation.

You can leave the mini lop rabbit in the room and be sure that he is playing and having a good time. Of course, this will totally depend on whether you can spare a room in the house or not.

2. Blocking off dangerous areas

There is no use to cry after the damage has been done. It is always better to take the necessary precautions in the very beginning. You should understand the various tendencies of the mini lop rabbit that can pose harm to him.

It is always a good idea to block off dangerous areas. This will mean that the mini lop rabbit will not be able to enter these areas, and you will be able to avoid any kind of mishaps.

You can use barriers to make sure that the mini lop rabbit can't reach certain spots and rooms in the house. But, a point that needs to be noted here is that good quality barriers will have to be used.

You should know that a mini lop rabbit can jump a long distance. So, blocking off areas should be done keeping this in mind. While they can easily jump off bookshelves, they can also squeeze behind one.

Puppy pens and baby gates are two options that you can consider while you are looking for ways to block off certain areas of the house. You can easily find them online or from a store.

Make sure that you make a list of all the areas in the house that you want to block from the bunny. You can choose to block a complete room or certain sections. You should know where you don't want your pet.

It is a good idea to make sure that the barriers are made of good quality metal. This will ensure that the bunny can't chew on it. The last thing that you would want is the mini lop chewing off the barriers that were meant to block him.

You should make sure that the right kinds of barriers are used. This is because your naughty mini lop rabbit will happily climb small barriers. He might even get his head stuck in the barrier openings, inviting more trouble for himself and for you also.

If you don't want to invest on high end barriers, then you can look for cheaper alternatives. You can find different kinds of barriers online. Or, you could get these barriers from a shop. They will help to solve your purpose and will be easier on your pocket.

These barriers have a very strong base of plastic. The plastic is good quality and also non-toxic. Barriers made of Plexiglas will also serve the purpose right.

You can make safe and secure barriers on your own. If you wish to make the barrier at your home, then you can use wood. Make sure that you understand how you need to make them.

You can also take some measures to keep the pet bunny away from your furniture. This is important so that they don't try to create a tunnel by chewing on the fabric.

You can also use a good piece of cardboard as a barrier. You can fix some heavy material of cardboard at the bottom end of the furniture that you are trying to protect. This is a relatively non expensive way of protecting your furniture.

To keep the rabbit away from the fridge or refrigerator, you can fix the cardboard in the opening. This will prevent the pet from entering the opening. Make sure you use a good quality cardboard.

This can prevent the pet from digging on the material of the furniture. You can also keep such barriers in front of various rooms. This will make sure that the pet can't enter these rooms. These are simple ways to keep the pet safe and also your things safe.

If you have recliners in your house, keep them away from the pet. The pet could be severely injured by these reclining chairs. The reclining action and the spring could injure the pet, especially the younger bunnies.

To be on the safer side, always check the chair or sofa that you are about to sit on. You don't want to sit on your bunny and injure him. Make sure he is not hiding under tables and sofas.

3. Keeping the mini lop away from house plants

You might be shocked to know that many varieties of plants are actually toxic to mini lop rabbits. Your rabbit doesn't know this and he mind end up eating the most toxic plants.

Plants such as tulips and holly are extremely toxic for the Mini lop rabbit. There are many other house plants that are poisonous for the Mini lop. You should try to keep the bunny away from all kinds of house plants.

The best thing to do will obviously be to keep the plats in an area where the pet mini lop rabbit can't reach them. This is a fool proof way to keep them away from the plants.

If you find your beloved pet chewing on a house plant, you should stop him from doing so. It is a good idea to take him to the vet immediately to make sure that he is safe and sound.

4. Keeping dangerous things off limits

If you observe the pet closely, you will start understanding his likes and preferences. After you have kept an eye on him for a few days, you will start understanding his favourite spots in the house.

You will know which areas he likes to dig and where he prefers to hide. These pieces of information can help you to bunny proof your home in a better way.

To begin with, you should make sure that all liquid chemicals are far away from the mini lop rabbit. If a chemical is in reach of the pet, he might accidently spill it all over him.

The bunny can even drink the chemical accidentally. Make sure that the bottles are always closed. To make sure that nothing of the sort happens, you should make sure that all such supplies are kept in top cabinets that the pet can't reach.

Keep your shoes in a cupboard or cabinet. Before you know, your rabbit might start chewing them. You should also check the bedding, furniture and other things on a regular basis.

You would be surprised to know that your pet can climb cabinets and cupboards. He might jump from high surfaces and might hurt himself in the process. You need to make sure that the rabbit is not up to such mischief.

You should also make sure that all kind of medicines, syrups and tablets are out of the reach of the mini lop rabbit. The pet might just swallow a tablet that it finds on the ground or table. He will not know that this is potential danger.

These can be very harmful for the pet. You can also get childproof cabinets in your home to keep all such potentially dangerous stuff in those cabinets.

You should also exercise precaution near toilets and washrooms. The mini lop rabbit can easily climb toilet seats and cabinets. Just imagine what can happen if the seat is not kept down.

The rabbit can slip or jump inside and can get himself hurt. To avert any such incident, make sure that he toilet seat is kept down. This should be especially done when the mini lop is around the toilet area.

You can also keep the toilet door closed to make sure that he does not enter the toilet. If there are any areas of the house that the pet needs to keep away from, you have to keep them closed and blocked. If you don't do so, the pet can just enter the space when you are not around.

The bunny might accidentally swallow the small or shredded pieces. Make sure that the toys that you allow the pet to play with are of good quality. They should be safe for the rabbit, and they should be impossible to swallow for the mini lop.

Rubber items can also be very dangerous if they are swallowed by the pet animal. Imagine the kind of damage a rubber band can do if the pet swallows it. You should know that the pet will not know what he is not supposed to do.

You will have to keep him away from danger. You might take some time figuring out to do things, but once you have it sorted, it will only get easier from there.

Your mini lop rabbit could actually shock you with the kind of things it can get hurt from. He might hurt himself while hopping from one chair to another or while chewing things.

You should make sure any such potentially dangerous things are out of the reach of the bunny. Keep the waste bin and waste stuff away from him because he might try to play with things that could be harmful for him.

You should make sure that the pet sleeps in his cage. This is for his safety and also for the good of the family members. You can also keep him in the cage when you can't supervise him and his actions.

You should make sure that the pet plays with the right kind of toys. Cheap plastic materials that can have an adverse effect on the health of the pet must be avoided. Similarly, toys that can be shredded or broken should also be avoided.

This might be very difficult for you in the beginning to look into areas and places that have hidden dangers for the pet. But, you will definitely learn with time and experience.

The furniture in the house should be pet-friendly. You should make sure there are no sharp edges that could hurt the animal. This will help the bunny to be safe when he is playing around.

Your mini lop rabbit could climb onto the washing machine and dish washer. So, make sure that these items always have a lid on. To be on the safer side, always check inside the washing machine and the dish washer before operating them.

The pet rabbit should stay away from the plants of the house. You should also make sure that he stays away from Styrofoam products. The pet could bite into them and swallow them. This can be potentially very dangerous.

Keep away all rubber products so that the pet can't reach them. This includes both soft rubber and foam rubber products. They can be very harmful if the pet swallows them.

You should also make sure that soaps and detergents are kept away from the reach of the pet. These items can be very dangerous for the pet. The mini lop rabbit could climb up counters and reach such things.

It is better to use the cabinets of bathrooms and rooms to keep things away from the pet rabbit. This will ensure that the pet can't reach them and can't harm himself.

You should make sure that the pet stays away from your clothes. He might chew them. Always keep the clothes in the cupboards. Never leave them lying around the house. This is like an invitation for the bunny.

Keep the cupboards locked and keep the laundry area closed and locked. If the rabbit gets inside a stack of clothes, it will be a party for him. He will dig tunnels and chew things.

5. Fencing

As a rabbit owner, you should also understand the importance of fencing the habitat of the rabbit. If the rabbit is kept in a cage that is kept inside the house at all times, then you can skip the need to fence. However, if you plan to leave the rabbit in an open space for longer durations, fencing is a must.

Fencing is also good for owners that have more than one rabbit. You could keep your rabbits in the open for longer durations of time without the fear of them being attacked. The rabbits could play and keep themselves entertained in the open spaces.

Fencing is a fundamental requirement when you keep your rabbit in your backyard or in an open land surrounded by wild animals. There have been many incidents with many rabbit owners where their rabbits have been attacked by wild animals.

If you have a pet, it can be extremely disturbing to find out that your beloved pet animal has been killed or taken away by predators. If you have a large number of rabbits on a farm for showing or other commercial purposes, this is definitely a huge economic loss.

It is important that the fencing is sturdy and well planned. A big animal such as a fox or dog can get over a fence that is about 5 feet in height. You will have to choose an enclosure based on the kind of predators that you are trying to ward off.

Preventing predators

The common predators that can pose danger to your pet rabbit or rabbits are dogs, foxes, badgers and cats. It is also known that weasels, snakes, ferrets and raccoons can act as deadly predators for the rabbits.

If you live in a place that is inhabited by any of these animals then you will face the issue of keeping the predator away. You should never underestimate a predator like a fox. Though they look and are perceived to be similar to dogs, they can climb over a fence or just jump over it very easily if they want to get to your rabbit. The options that you have with respect to fences to prevent predators are as follows:

Electric netting: This is an ideal type of fencing provided there is no chance of a short circuit because of long grass. You must also avoid this fencing in areas that have children playing in it. If your area is suitable for electric netting, it is the best option as it is portable and can be moved to areas where the rabbit has access to fresh grass.

Triple wire fencing: This is a secure form of low fencing that can also include an electrical wire at the base. This will prevent any digging and will stop predators that will climb over it as well.

Improving security

If your area has foxes as the main predators, the fence should be buried deep into the ground to make sure that digging is not an option. It will also need to be tall enough to prevent the predator from climbing over.

There are several quality grades for the wiring. Getting strong netting will also ensure that the predator cannot tear through the fence. If you notice that the predator is trying to tear through the fence, it is a good idea to double it up to the height that the predator can tear through.

A large fox can be kept out if your fence is about 6 feet in height. Turning the top upwards and running an electric strand on top will also help prevent any climbing. Make sure that the electric strand is high enough to keep children from reaching it. In places that have a high incidence of fox attacks, a fence that is less than 5 meters is not recommended.

Foxes are known to dig through areas where the ground is soft. Badgers are also extremely good at digging and tearing the net apart. If this is the primary issue that you are facing, it is a good idea to have the fencing buried up to about 8 inches into the ground.

Areas with clay soil are not susceptible to digging. On the other hand, if you have sandy soil, you will have to bury the fence as deep as you can. You should remember that any ground that humans can dig into easily will be easy for foxes and badgers.

You can even turn the fence up after 8 inches of burying it. Covering the turned up area with rubble and bricks is a great idea. Additionally, you can even cover the wire with soil after it has been dug in.

If badgers are the primary predator, overlaying the fence with an extra layer of netting or having triple wire is a good idea. This will ensure that strong predators like badgers stay out. Adding an electric wire at the height of the nose of the badger will also help immensely.

Patching the fence up with gravel boards at the bottom is also a good idea. This means that the predator will have to dig deeper to get through. You can also turn the wire out. You may have to peg the wire down after laying the wire on the surface of the ground for about 24 inches.

The action of the earthworms will help the fence sink in deeper. You will also notice that the grass will grow through the wire.

Netting options

Chicken netting is quite useful to protect an enclosed area. This type of netting is also called rabbit wire as it is used to keep rabbits from digging through and getting to crops. This net can keep off predators such as dogs and foxes.

There are various grades of chicken netting. Across the widest part of the gap or hole in the fence, the netting is about 50mm. These wires are galvanized to make sure that they do not rust.

You can get cheaper nets that are 2, 3, 4 and 6 feet in width or about 10, 25 and 50 meters lengthwise. If the predator in your area is a fox, you will need to get netting that will allow you to dig it in at least up to 18 inches while allowing ample height to prevent the predator from getting in.

Agricultural merchants will be able to sell chicken netting to you. You will also be able to find several suppliers online. Buying online is a cheaper option most of the time as there are regular deals and offers for you to look out for.

If you don't have foxes in your area, you can also opt for portable netting. These nets are meant to keep various pets in a specific area and are not used for predators. This is ideal even when you want to restrain the rabbit when you are introducing a new pet in the household.

Fencing a large area

If you have a large area that you have to enclose, a low electric fence is a good idea. With most predators, the first step is for them to investigate the fence to look for the easiest way in. While doing this, if the electric fence even touches their nose, they will not attempt to get close to it.

You also have the option of sheep or pig fencing. This can be installed by a contractor. Although these fences are lower, the option of adding electrical wires makes it the most economical option available to you. The only thing you need to make sure is that the grass does not cut the electric connection, rendering it ineffective.

Of course, fencing is the first step to protecting your pet. You must also make sure that you keep the pet inside the housing area every night. This housing must be locked to keep the pet additionally secure. If you are unable to lock the housing area each night, getting an automatic door is a good idea, as it can be timed as per your convenience.

Chapter 6: Maintaining health of the mini lop rabbit

It is very important that you invest your time and energy in understanding the health requirements of the rabbit. This will allow your pet rabbit to enjoy a happier and healthier life.

There are a few diseases to which a mini lop rabbit is susceptible. An understanding of the symptoms and precautions of these diseases will help you to avoid them.

It should be understood that sometimes a rabbit can suffer for a very long time from a particular disease. This will make it very difficult to treat him later. No symptom should be ignored. You should take the pet animal to a veterinarian even at the slightest doubt.

This chapter will help you to understand how you can keep your pet healthy. You will be able to understand the symptoms, precautions and cure of common diseases that can affect your pet animal.

1. Understanding symptoms at an early stage

It is a known fact that the earlier you catch the symptoms of a disease, the higher the chances are to treat it. Often many symptoms go unnoticed, leading to serious complications and issues in the future for the pet.

The first way to catch symptoms at an early stage is to spend quality time with the pet. This will allow you to understand the mannerisms and behavior of your pet in a better light. Even the slightest deviation from this usual behavior should be taken as a warning signal.

Rabbits all over the world are susceptible to various diseases. Some of these diseases are more common than others, and most of them can be very dangerous if necessary precautions are not taken.

It should be noted that even if your pet is healthy and all seems to be just fine with him, you should make sure that you take him to the vet for periodic visits.

The vet will examine the health of the pet rabbit and will help you to understand if something needs your attention. As with humans, an early detected problem or disease can be treated easily in pets.

There are a few symptoms that will help you to identify stress and sickness in your pet. Examine the behavior and the body of the pet carefully.

You should never ignore any symptom that you see because an ignored symptom will lead to serious problems later.

The following signs can help you to understand that there is something wrong with the pet rabbit:

- **Respiratory**: You should pay attention to the breathing of the pet animal. If the pet is having difficulty breathing, this could be an obvious symptom of some disease.

- **Nose**: The sick pet could be snoring very loudly while making noises from is nose. There could be some discharge from the nose.

- **Eating disorders**: He will lose his appetite. The pet will lose an interest in eating and drinking. This is a signal that something is definitely wrong with the pet. If the animal is not treated on time, you will see that his appetite decreases with time. It will decrease to a point that it will become difficult for the animal to carry on his daily tasks. The rabbit could also show the symptom of diarrhea. He will suffer from frequent and liquid stools.

- **Mobility**: A sick rabbit will appear as if he is out of balance. He will be fidgety in his movements. In some cases, the rabbit might not even have the strength to walk.

- **Coat of the animal**: A dull coat is also an indication of a sick pet. The quality of the fur or the coat directly represents the health of the pet. If the pet is losing too much hair, even that could be an indication.

- **Eyes**: The eyes could be swollen or have discharge.

- **Ears**: The ears could be swollen or could have visibly drooped.

As soon as you spot any of the symptoms, take the pet rabbit to a qualified and good veterinarian. He/she will be able to confirm the presence of disease and stress in the animal.

If you find your pet behaving different from normal, then the first step you should take is to provide him warmth. It is important that the pet is not cold and that the proper temperature is maintained.

You should try to make the pet feel secure and safe when he is stressed. You should keep him securely on a comfortable blanket to make him feel easy and comfortable.

You should make sure that your pet can rest well in a calm environment. Keep him away from other animals. Make sure that there are no noises around the rabbit. Discourage your family members from gathering around the pet. This will stress him more.

It is important that you are able to identify the signs of emergency in your pet so that you can act without delay.

2. How to prevent diseases

While you are learning about the various diseases, their symptoms and cure, it is also important to learn about simple ways to prevent disease.

You should make sure that your pet is always kept in a clean environment. A neat and clean environment will help you to ward off many common ailments and diseases.

The food that the animal eats, the conditions around him and the care and love that you give him will all affect the general well being and the health of the rabbit.

You should also make sure that the pet is well fed at all times. Low quality food and insufficient food can also lead to health-related issues in the pet.

There are many issues that might not start as a big problem, but become serious problems if not treated on time. If you can detect a disease at an early stage, there are more chances that the disease will be cured.

Apart from this, you should take him for regular check-ups to the veterinarian. You should always consult a veterinarian when you find any unusual traits and symptoms in the pet.

It is important to control and prevent diseases in your pet animal. The pet should be examined completely before you buy him from the breeder. Make sure that you only opt for reliable sources when it comes to breeders. This is a simple way to ensure that your pet starts out healthy. Such a pet has stronger chances to overcome various diseases.

Make sure that your pet has access to regular vaccinations and medicines. You must always give them medicines and vaccinations only after you have consulted a veterinarian. You should never experiment with their health. Wrong medication can lead to serious issues.

If you find a pet unwell, make sure that you isolate him immediately. This should be done until the condition improves because there is no way of knowing if it can harm your other pets in any way. This will help to keep the other pets safe and disease free.

In case of any death, ensure that the rabbit that is dead is incinerated or buried properly. It is also recommended that you get a diagnostic report at the earliest. The samples from the carcass can be sent to the vet to determine the cause of the rabbit's death.

If you have visitors in your house regularly, make sure that they do not meet the sick rabbit without any protective clothing. This is to help the rabbit get better and also to avoid making these people carriers of disease.

Taking some precautions can help you save a lot of money that you may have to spend on medical bills and veterinarian services otherwise. This is important so that even the smallest health issue can be tracked at an early stage. Prevention is always better than cure.

Identifying and treating injuries in mini lop rabbits

An unhealthy pet can be a nightmare for any owner. You might be thinking about what you can do to ensure that the pet is always in the prime of its health. You can contribute a great deal to the health of the animal.

When you are looking to maintain the health of your pet mini lop rabbit, then you should make an attempt to understand the common health issues that the animal faces. This will help you to prepare yourself well and also treat your pet well.

It is important that you take care of your pet's health. The pet will depend on you for most of its needs. It will not be able to tell you if it is facing any discomfort regarding its health. You should be able to identify the symptoms of various diseases in your pet to treat it well.

You should also be able to diagnose any symptoms of injuries in your pet. If you can treat him in your home, then you should do it very carefully. In case you have any doubts, you should take the pet to the veterinarian.

As you would have understood by now, your mini lop rabbit is a very mischievous animal. He will lead a very active lifestyle. The pet likes hopping and jumping around. He will also enjoy exploring things around him.

All the traits of the bunny make it susceptible to many injuries. There is nothing to worry about if your pet animal injures itself. You should be able to diagnose the injuries so that they can be treated well.

Never commit the mistake of ignoring an injury or symptom. Even if you have the slightest doubt, you should always act on it. It is always a good idea to take the mini lop rabbit to the veterinarian if you spot something unnatural with the pet.

It is important that you learn the basics of diagnosing the injuries. This is important because if a small injury is treated well, the mini lop rabbit can be saved from a major problem in the future.

You should be on the lookout for any symptoms that your mini lop rabbit might display when it is injured. These symptoms could mean that there is something wrong with your bunny.

It is important that you understand that your pet animal might not show any signs of injuries, even when it is injured. It will be your responsibility to diagnose the injury before it turns into a bigger problem.

Understand some basic signs of injuries, stress and diseases in the pet mini lop rabbit. This will help you to get the pet treated on time. If the pet is treated on time, you can avoid many future problems.

Is your pet looking very lazy and lethargic? Is your mini lop rabbit looking very disturbed? This could be because he has injured himself and is in pain.

The pet might injure himself with a chair or other furniture while playing. The limbs of the animal could also be hanging. This is also a clear sign of injury to the pet. You should closely examine his limbs to be sure.

Is your pet stumbling? Is the pet showing uncoordinated movements? If you find these symptoms, then you know that the pet has some issues. Take him on your lap and gently check his limbs.

If there is a change in the way he sits or stands or carries himself, then this could also mean that the injury has forced the pet to change the way he usually is. This could be because he is in pain.

You should look out for the faeces of the animal. If there is any change in the colour of the faeces, this could mean that there is something wrong with the health of the pet.

Do you witness any changes in the skin of the pet? If yes, then this could also mean that there is something that needs your attention. Don't overlook anything that does not seem natural.

Do you spot any blood on the skin of the animal? Does the fur of the pet look different? You should look for blood stains in the enclosure of the animal also. This could mean that something is not right. Look for certain common symptoms, such as coughing and vomiting by the animal.

If your pet looks scared and tense, you should understand that it is for a reason. You need to closely examine him to find out what is wrong.

When you spot any of the given symptoms in your pet, you should know that something is not right. You will have to take a closer look at the pet and examine. This examination will help you to understand if there is something wrong with your pet.

While you are examining your pet, you should also understand that your pet could be scared. It is important that you make the pet feel comfortable. This will help you conduct the examination properly and without any problems.

To make sure that the pet animal is not terrified when you are trying to examine him for any potential injuries, you should make sure that you conduct the examination in a closed area, a place where the animal feels safe and protected. You should try to examine him indoors.

Make sure that all the tools that are needed for the examination are ready. You shouldn't leave your pet alone to fetch the tools. Everything should be ready before the examination.

The noise level around you should be as low as possible. The noise will stress the pet and will irritate him, so make sure there is no noise around. Conduct the examination in a quiet place. This is important to keep things under control.

Do not let the place be crowded when the examination is being conducted. Make sure that all the other pets and your family members are outside and not in the same place where the examination is being conducted.

If the animal sees you being fidgety, it will only add to his stress. Be as gentle and kind as possible. This will help your pet to relax and feel less stressed. You should in no way add to the stress and pain of the pet.

You should be as calm and as confident as possible. Your confidence will give him some hope and relief. These are some very simple tips, but will go a long way in ensuring that the pet is being handled well.

You should check his entire body. Remember to check on both sides of the body. Start the examination at one particular point and then move ahead from that point. The examination should be definite and guided and not random.

Look at how your pet responds to the body examination being done. If you feel that the animal is not taking it too well, you should stop the examination. You should look for any stress signs that he displays.

It is important that you don't ignore any symptoms. It is also important that you don't force anything on the pet; otherwise the animal can go into deep shock. After your initial check-up, if you find something wrong then visit the veterinarian.

You should never self-treat the pet. This could complicate things further. Take the pet to the veterinarian because he is the best judge of the pet's condition. Discuss your doubts and confusions with the vet.

Veterinary care

If you wish to keep your mini lop rabbit happy and healthy, you need specialized veterinary care to do so. While a regular vet will be able to provide you with temporary relief during an emergency, you will need a qualified veterinarian that practices medicine on rabbits.

You need to find a veterinarian that understands your concern for your pet rabbit. So, when you are in talks with a vet who can potentially become the one to take care of your rabbit, remember to discuss your doubts with him/her.

Don't wait for the pet to fall sick. It is always a good idea to choose a veterinarian for the animal in advance. If your pet falls sick or encounters an injury, you should know where to take him. The last thing you want to do is to search for a vet when the pet's condition is deteriorating.

The best way to find a good veterinarian is to go by the breeder's suggestion. A good breeder will always consult a good vet, and will suggest the same to you.

It is important that the veterinarian has good experience of working with bunnies. Many of them might have the knowledge, but might lack in practical experience. It is your duty to make sure that the vet holds a good name amongst other owners of rabbits.

While you are choosing your veterinarian, you should also consider the distance of the clinic and your home. You would want to consult a vet who is good and also close to your home.

3. Common diseases in mini lop rabbits

This section will help you to understand the various common health problems that your pet rabbit can suffer from. As the caregiver, you should attempt to understand these diseases in detail so that you can provide the animal with the right care.

Pasteurellosis

Mini lop rabbits are prone to Pasteurellosis. It is one of the most common diseases known to affect rabbits across various species. It is also known as sniffles.

It can be controlled easily with the help of a few precautions and measures. Once the pet acquires this disease, it keeps spreading if the condition is not treated.

Cause

The cause of Pasteurellosis or sniffles is a bacterium that is known as Pasteurella multocida. This bacterium attacks the respiratory system of mini lop rabbits.

It is also known that there are different strains of this bacterium. These strains can have a deadly effect on various parts of the rabbit's body, such as ears and the eyes.

If this disease spreads to the eyes of the mini lop rabbit, he can acquire Conjunctivitis. On the other hand, if this disease spreads to the ears of the mini lop rabbit, he can experience head tilting and severe disorientation.

Symptoms

It should be noted that the symptoms of the disease will depend on the strain of bacteria that affects the rabbit. You can look out for the following general symptoms in the rabbit to know if he is suffering from this particular disease:

- The animal will have a runny nose. This is one of the first symptoms of the disease.

- The animal will sneeze a lot.

- If you go near the animal, you will hear him snoring or sniffling while he breathes.

- The rabbit can experience sores or abscesses on his respiratory tract. This will also be very painful.

- He can experience head tilting and severe disorientation.

Treatment

This particular disease can be controlled easily with the help of antibiotics. You should consult a veterinarian as soon as you catch the symptoms of the disease. It should be noted that ignored symptoms can lead to a severe case of Pasteurellosis.

The veterinarian will keep the pet rabbit on a supplementary biotic and antibiotic course for the duration of four to about thirty days. This will depend on the severity of the disease.

Calcivirus

Calcivirus is also known as VHD or viral haemorrhagic disease. Calcivirus is more prevalent in the wild rabbits. It is a viral disease, which can turn extremely lethal if not treated on time.

Cause

The disease is caused by a virus, as the name itself suggests. It can affect the lymph nodes in a very drastic way. In severe cases, the liver can be completely damaged.

If the disease is allowed to spread, it will affect the blood of the animal. The blood will not coagulate. This in turn will affect many other organs of the pet animal.

Symptoms

The following symptoms will help you to confirm whether your pet is suffering from this health condition:

- The virus can lead to inflammation of the intestine, which gets worse with time if it is not treated.

- The pet will also experience a high fever.

- As the disease progresses, the pet will lose his energy and will appear more and more lethargic.

Treatment

If you notice any of the given symptoms in your pet rabbit, you should take him to the veterinarian. He/she will take a blood sample of the animal and test it for the disease, along with other tests.

Though the disease can be controlled to some extent, there is no specific treatment for this particular disease. It is suggested to sanitize the habitat of the pet thoroughly, as maintaining hygiene will help to keep this disease-causing virus away from the pet rabbit.

Scours

Scours is one of the most common diseases known to affect rabbits across various species. This condition is characterized by excessive diarrhea in the rabbits.

This is a bacterial disease and can be controlled easily with the help of a few precautions. If you give your bunny a proper and healthy diet and also try to maintain optimal hygiene conditions around him, you can definitely avoid this health condition in the pet.

Cause

The main reasons behind scours are unhealthy diet and poor hygiene conditions. If the pet is suffering from a severe case of viral or bacterial infection, scours could be one of the side effects of the infection. In such cases, it is best to treat the infection if you want to treat this condition.

Another common cause of this health condition in bunnies is stress and over-heating. When your pet is going through excessive stress, it will lead to scours.

If there is poor hygiene around the pet, it can also lead to scours. You should try to maintain optimum hygiene levels at all times. If the pet is suffering from some other infection or health condition, scours could be a side effect of the health condition.

Symptoms

The following symptoms will help you to confirm whether your pet is suffering from this health condition:

- One of the early symptoms of this disease includes diarrhea. If your pet is suffering from diarrhea that you are not able to control, then your pet could be suffering from scours.

- You should keep a check on the stools of the rabbit. The color and texture of the stools will help you determine whether the rabbit has scours or not.

Treatment

If your pet rabbit is suffering from excessive diarrhea or scours, you would have to take certain measures to solve this issue. He should be given electrolytes. The electrolytes will help to give the body the salts that it might have lost because of the condition.

It is advised to administer probiotics to the animal. This will help to treat his condition.

Once your pet starts getting better, you should make sure that it is given a very healthy diet. A good diet can prevent scours. You can even consult your veterinarian if your pet doesn't get better. The medication given by the doctor will help the pet to get better soon.

Make sure that all the necessary nutrients are given to the pet. You can also look to give him supplements if his diet does not provide the right nutrition.

Infestation with mites

Mini lop rabbits are also prone to mites. Mites can lead to skin irritation in the beginning and then severe skin allergy if not treated.

It is not a very deadly disease and can be controlled easily with the help of a few precautions and measures. Once the pet acquires this disease, it keeps spreading if the condition is not treated.

Symptoms

You can look out for the following symptoms in the rabbit to know that he is suffering from this particular disease:

- Inflammation of the skin because of the infection caused by mites makes the pet irritable and restless.

- It is a skin disease, so a change in the texture of the skin on the pet could be an indication of an infection. In most cases, the skin starts getting red.

- You will notice dandruff patches on the skin of the rabbit. You should look at the nape of the neck and the base of the animal's tail, where the patches will be very prominent.

- As the condition worsens, the patch size will increase.

- The pet will scratch again and again at one spot. You will find the pet to be very irritated and agitated. The skin could also develop rashes or scales.

Treatment

The skin disease can be treated by the use of mild medicated soaps. These soaps will soothe the skin and will also treat the infection.

There are some creams that can also help to treat the skin and make the condition better. In severe cases, certain ointments might have to be applied to the skin. You should also take care of the diet of the pet.

A good diet will help the skin to heal itself faster. In case the skin gets worse with time then you will have to consult the veterinarian. He might suggest some oral medicines to heal the skin faster.

He might also suggest some special ointments that will give some relief to the pet. The use of 'Ivermectin' is recommended for the rabbits. It helps the skin to get rid of mites faster.

It is also suggested to clean the habitat of the pet after the pet is treated. This is to avoid any relapse of the skin disease.

You should also focus on grooming the animal. This also helps the animal to get rid of dead cells, thus lowering the chance of an infestation of mites.

Urine burn

Urine burn is also common in rabbits. When the urine of the rabbit soaks the fur, it leads to this particular condition.

This can further lead to inflammation of the skin, which gets worse with time if it is not treated. The pet will also experience severe hair loss.

Symptoms

You can look out for the following symptoms in the rabbit to know whether he is suffering from this particular disease:

- Inflammation of the skin because of the infection makes the pet irritable and restless.

- His private areas will appear sore and red. This is one of the most common symptoms of the disease.

Treatment

The burn can be treated by the use of mild medicated soaps. These soaps will soothe the skin and will also treat the infection.

There are some soothing creams and ointments that can help to treat the skin and make the condition better. You should also take care of the diet of the pet.

In case the skin gets worse with time, then you will have to consult the veterinarian, who may suggest oral medicine.

It is also suggested to keep the habitat of the pet clean. This is to avoid any relapse of the skin disease. The cage needs to be dry and clean at all times.

Pneumonia

The rabbit is also highly susceptible to pneumonia, especially when the bunny is young. If your bunny shows symptoms of a respiratory disorder, you should look for various symptoms of this disease.

It can be caused by bacteria of a virus that thrives in dirty and unsanitary conditions. This is the reason why it is always advised to keep the hutches clean and sanitary.

The main cause of this health condition is damp hutches and cages. If the living conditions of the pet are not good, he can suffer from this disease.

It is important that you treat this disease because it is known to be a life-threating condition. If you discover any respiratory disorders in your pet, you should take the issue seriously because as the disease reaches its advanced stages, it becomes more difficult to treat.

Symptoms

You should be on the lookout for the following symptoms to confirm the presence of the disease in your rabbit:

- If your pet animal refuses to eat, then this could be because of this disease. The pet will suffer a drastic loss of appetite.

- Is your pet being very lazy and lethargic? Is he refusing to move? This could also be because of this disease.

- The pet will have difficulty breathing. There could be a blockage or congestion in the chest area. This is a very common symptom and should be taken very seriously.

- The pet could be suffering from high temperature. This is also a very common symptom accompanying pneumonia.

- The pet might vomit the food that he is fed. This is because of the congestion in his chest.

Treatment

There is treatment available if your rabbit is suffering from pneumonia. The type of treatment that will be chosen will depend on a few factors. If the pneumonia is too severe, then a different treatment is chosen in comparison to if it is not too severe.

The vet will recommend antibiotics to combat the disease. The dose and strength of the antibiotic will depend on the severity of pneumonia in the pet bunny.

If the bunny is not able to recover and is already at an advanced stage, then the dose of antibiotic is injected directly through the skin. This is known to work rapidly on the animal.

Ringworm

Ringworms are a very common issue that can affect your pet rabbit. Ringworms can attach themselves to the rabbit. This will cause immense discomfort to the rabbit.

While many people don't consider this as a major health issue, ringworms should never be ignored. They are known to be very dangerous. They can be a potential threat to your other pets as well. You should make sure that ringworms are treated well and on time.

If you believe that ringworm is a worm, then you are wrong. It is a fungus and fungal treatment is required to get rid of ringworms. If you are treating your pet for worms, then you will not be able to combat this condition.

The problem with this disease is that it can get worse with time, so it is important that you treat it as soon as possible. If ringworms are allowed to grow on the animal, they will lead to a lot of fur loss.

Causes

There are many causes that could be behind the ringworms attacking your pet. One of the most common causes of ringworms is contact with animals already infested with the same.

Ringworms can easily travel from one carrier to another, so if an animal infested with ringworms comes into contact with your bunny, he can easily get them too.

Symptoms

You should be on the lookout for the following symptoms to confirm the presence of ringworms on your rabbit:

- Is your rabbit scratching itself too much? Does your pet seem as if he has an itch? Do you see some areas red with itchiness and scratching?

- Do you find him irritable and uneasy? If the answer is yes, then your rabbit could be infected with ringworms.

- Ringworms make the animal itchy and too much itchiness can develop red sores on the body. You should be on the lookout for such obvious symptoms of ringworms.

- The pet will slowly develop bald patches. You should be on the lookout for this symptom. It is one of the most common symptoms of the rabbit being infected with ringworms.

- The head of the bunny is most likely to be affected. It will slowly spread to other parts of the body. You should look out for bald patches on the head.

Treatment

If you find the given symptoms on your pet then you can be convinced that your pet has been infested with ringworms. It is important that you take the steps to help your pet get rid of them.

If you do not treat the pet soon, then they will only trouble the poor animal more. You can successfully treat them by following an antifungal treatment for the disease.

You should not allow the pet to come into contact with other pets of the house. The ringworms can spread very easily. Human beings can also easily catch them. You should wear gloves when you go near the pet.

If you find any of the above symptoms in a rabbit, it is important that you waste no time and take the pet to the veterinarian. The vet will conduct some tests to confirm the condition.

He/she will suggest an antifungal cream that will help to get rid of the ringworms. The hair or fur in the affected area needs to be tied so that the ringworms don't spread to other parts of the body.

Hair loss

Another common problem that your mini lop rabbit can go through is hair loss. Though this might not seem like a big problem, hair loss is generally an indication of other serious problems. Therefore, it is important that you don't take the issue lightly. You should make an attempt to understand the causes of hair loss so that you can work on eliminating those issues.

If your rabbit is very young, hair loss could be an indication that your pet has been kept in extremely warm temperatures. The young pet might not be taking the warm environment well.

If your mini lop rabbit is not too young, then hair loss could be an effect of some other health issue. You should understand these issues. The most common reasons behind hair loss are unhealthy diet and too much stress.

Causes

One of the most common causes of hair loss in mini lop rabbits is lack of a healthy diet. You have to make sure that your pet is fed properly so that it can be in its optimum health and glory.

Another common cause of hair loss in mini lop rabbits is stress. The first things that you should look into after you spot hair loss are the diet and the stress levels of your pet. Apart from these two common causes, there are a few other causes of hair loss in the animal. If your pet is facing some skin allergy or has skin irritation, it can lead to hair loss.

It is also known that fungal infections lead to drastic hair loss. If your pet has suffered from some fungal infection in the recent past, then this could be the cause of hair loss in the pet.

Sometimes, a large amount of bleach is present in soap items. This bleach is harmful for the mini lop rabbit. You should also check the amount of bleach that is present in the soap that is used to wash things that often come into direct contact with your pet. For example, you can check the amount of bleach present in the soap powder that is used to wash the water container and the food container of your mini lop rabbit.

Symptoms

The most obvious symptom of hair loss in an animal is the reduction of hair on the body. You might spot hair all over the place.

-    If you spot a bald patch on your mini lop rabbit, then your pet has been suffering from hair loss.

-    You should also look for hair loss in bigger and larger areas.

Treatment

If you spot hair loss in your mini lop rabbit, you should immediately look for the direct or indirect causes behind the same. There can be many causes of hair loss, thus the treatment accordingly varies.

You should make a thorough check on the living conditions of the pet. This will help you to understand the problems that he is facing and the causes behind the hair loss. You might be required to make changes and adjustments on the basis your evaluation. If the cause of the hair loss is food related, then make sure that you work on providing the pet with a wholesome and nutritious diet.

If the cause behind the hair loss is a fungal infection, then you have to make sure that the infection is treated and eliminated. You should apply suitable anti-fungal topical creams for treating the fungal infection well.

If the mini lop rabbit is stressed, then the most obvious treatment to reduce and stop hair loss will be to reduce the stress of the mini lop rabbit. You would have to understand the reasons that could be behind the pet being so stressed. You will be required to make appropriate changes in the pet's living conditions to improve his health and reduce his stress levels.

Fleas or lice

As you might know, if an animal is infested with fleas or lice, it can get very difficult and uncomfortable for the animal. Fleas also lead to other issues and problems. Your mini lop rabbit can catch fleas or lice easily if it comes into contact with other domesticated animals. For example, if you have a pet dog or a pet cat along with the rabbit, then there is a strong chance that your rabbit caught the fleas from them.

Both fleas and lice are parasites that can irritate animals. It can be very easy for your pet to get these parasites, but the good news is that a common treatment can help you to get rid of both these parasites. Another important point that you need to understand is that even after you treat these parasites, the infection can re-occur. It is important to work on the cause of these annoying parasites.

Causes

One of the most common causes of infestation is the contact with animals already infested with the parasites.

Symptoms

The following symptoms will help you to confirm whether your pet is suffering from a parasite infestation:

- The skin of the pet will start to get red. Look for red spots on different areas of the pet. The red areas could also be swollen.

- Does your pet appear itchy? Is he irritated and annoyed? Is he itching more than usual? If the answer to all these questions is yes, then this could be a parasite infestation.

- Does the pet seem visibly irritated? The parasites will make the pet very irritable. He might seem like he is being very moody, but in actual fact it is the irritation caused by the fleas and the lice.

Treatment

If your rabbit is suffering from a parasite infestation by either fleas or lice, you don't need to worry, as it can be treated. You need to make sure that you work on the cause of the parasites also; otherwise the parasites can strike again.

If the other domestic animals in the house have passed on the infestation to the rabbit, then you should make sure that these pets are also treated for the parasite infestation. If you don't do so, there will be a second infestation.

Both fleas and lice can be treated with the same remedy. You would need to apply a special powder to the affected areas of the rabbit. The powder will cool down the area, repair the skin and will also help to disable the fleas and the lice so that they don't create any further damage.

The special powder that needs to be applied on the pet is pyrethrum or carbaryl powder. You can even consult your veterinarian if you think that the infestation is becoming serious.

Coccidiosis

One of the most common health problems in rabbits is the Coccidiosis. This particular health problem is caused by protozoa Cocci, which have only one single cell.

It is important to know that there are nine types of Cocci that can affect rabbits. Eight out of these nine types are known to affect the intestines of the bunnies. The ninth type of Cocci can affect the liver of the rabbit.

You should also know that cats, dogs and chickens can also be affected by Cocci. It is important to note that young rabbits are often more susceptible to Cocci.

Older bunnies have immunity against this disease, so if you have a young rabbit, then you should be worried about this health issue. It is important that you understand the causes and ways to avoid this disease.

Causes

One of the most common causes of this disease is an unclean enclosure. If the cage or the hutch of the rabbit is not cleaned for days, you can expect your rabbit to get infected with this disease.

The parasite will dwell in dirty areas. The rabbit will ingest the egg of the disease-causing parasite. They will do so when they lick or eat from dirty cage floors or when they eat contaminated hay.

While the adult rabbit is less likely to suffer from this condition, it can be a carrier. It can shed the eggs of the parasite in its feces. This can further infect other pet rabbits in the vicinity.

The eggs of this disease-causing parasite can thrive and survive for over a year in a humid and warm environment. This makes it all the more important that you regularly clean the surroundings of the rabbit.

Symptoms

You can look out for the following symptoms in the bunny to know whether he is suffering from this particular disease:

- The pet will lose his appetite. You will find him avoiding even his favorite foods. He will not drink water, which could further lead to dehydration.

- You will notice sudden and drastic weight loss in the pet. This is one of the most common symptoms of this condition.

- Another symptom of this disorder is vomiting. The pet will throw up from time to time.

- The pet would be seen struggling during his bowel movements. You should watch out for this symptom.

- You will notice the bunny being very lazy and lethargic.

- You can spot your rabbit sitting in one corner with a hunched back. His feet will be forward, and he will appear to be really sad and sick.

- The pet will suffer from diarrhea. You might also notice blood in the stools of the rabbit.

Treatment

If you find any of the above symptoms in a rabbit, it is important that you waste no time and take the pet to the veterinarian. The vet will conduct some tests to confirm the condition.

The most common treatment of this condition includes the use of corid powder. You can get it easily at all pet stores. Sulfamethoxide is also used to help the pet recover from this condition.

It should be mixed with water and given to the pet rabbit for seven days. After the first cycle, a break of over seven days is taken. After that, the mix needs to be given for another seven days.

Most veterinarians will suggest completing these two cycles at least once in six months. This ensures that the rabbit does not get this health condition again. This is all the more important in young bunnies.

If your female bunny is pregnant, you should not administer this particular drug to the doe. It can be given to her once she is in the lactating phase.

It is important that you don't ignore any symptoms and consult the vet as soon as possible. Always try to maintain cleanliness in the hutch of the pet rabbit.

Chapter 7: Training the mini lop rabbit

It is very important to train the animal to make him more suitable to a household. Give him some time and show some patience.

No matter how much you read about an animal, your pet will have some individual characteristics that will separate him from the rest of the lot. The training phase can be a great opportunity for you to learn more about your pet.

It may take weeks or months before you see any positive results. If you fail to be kind towards him during the training process, he will detest coming to you and things will only get worse.

Don't punish the rabbit if he fails to follow you. You should remember to have fun even during the training phase. You shouldn't be too harsh on your pet.

The pet might slip into sadness and depression if severe training sessions continue. This will hamper the pet's emotional bond with you and also his health.

Rabbits generally associate chasing with being held captive. When you are training the rabbit, try not to chase him.

If you wish to play with him, kneel on the floor. You should be on the same level as the rabbit if you want him to enjoy playing with you.

They will play in your arms for some time and then will want to come down. You should be prepared for such behavior from your pet.

1. Is it possible to train a mini lop rabbit?

It is imperative to train a pet. It is a way to monitor their behavior and to teach them what behavior is acceptable and what isn't. This is a simple way of helping him adapt to your home and your family.

Apart from teaching him the right behavior, training will also help to form a bond between you and your pet. It will bring the two of you closer to each other.

It is often believed that it is very difficult to train a mini lop rabbit because he is mischievous and playful. The truth is that it is possible to train the mini lop rabbit well with continuous efforts.

The sooner you start the training, the better. You should start the training when the rabbit is very young. In fact, you should start the training soon after you bring him home.

You should adopt simple training techniques to train your mini lop rabbit. If you are consistent, you will get very good results.

If you start the training of the pet from a young age then this will give the pet some time to learn and understand what is expected of him. It is also important that the training is not stopped at any stage. Once you see him picking it up, reduce the intensity but don't stop the training.

When you are training your pet animal, you need to teach him what is acceptable and what is not. It is important to send the right signals to the pet. This is a way of teaching him as to what is expected of him and what is not. The pet will take some time, but will soon understand your instructions.

If your pet tries to bite you continuously then you should give a small toy to the pet. Let him bite the toy. You should repeat this action whenever he tries to bite you. This will send a signal to the pet animal that it is not okay for him to bite you.

When you are looking at training the rabbit, you should be aiming for litter training and training against chewing and biting above everything else.

While you are training your pet, you should remember that the rabbit needs to feel comfortable and secure in your presence. He will only learn when he feels secure with you.

You should spend quality time with him. Don't put him in the cage just to punish him. This will send the wrong message.

If he is left in the cage unattended all the time, he might become very aggressive. This can encourage his chewing and biting behavior. Always remember that they can bite when they are scared and disappointed.

You should never neglect your pet. The rabbit will learn slowly, but you have to be compassionate and kind towards the pet. Treat him when he exhibits good behavior. This will encourage him further.

2. How to train the mini lop rabbit effectively

If you have a mini lop rabbit as a pet, you will need to spend a lot of time creating a bond between you. Mini lop rabbits are gentle creatures that make great companions. You can enrich this experience by trying to understand your pet and building a relationship with him.

In this chapter, you will learn how to communicate with your mini lop rabbit and also the possibilities with having a trained mini lop rabbit.

Understanding the body language of the bunny

The first step towards building a relationship with your pet is being able to communicate with him. In the case of all pets, verbal communication is the least important tool. What you must focus on mostly is the body language. That will help you figure out the mood and the emotions that your pet is trying to convey, which will make training a lot easier.

Approaching the mini lop rabbit

Communication can be initiated only when you are able to approach your pet confidently without causing any panic or negative experience for either of you. This section will discuss a few tips to approach a mini lop rabbit properly and safely.

Make sure that you start slow. Walk towards the mini lop rabbit slowly and keep the talking to a minimum. The only thing the mini lop rabbit will focus on is your body and the signals that you are giving out.

Stop at regular intervals and observe the mini lop rabbit. Does he look comfortable? Does he want to approach you himself? Is he trying to get away from you? If he is moving away, you must stand quietly and let him relax.

After a few moments of no activity, try to approach the mini lop rabbit again. Make sure that your hands are lowered. Your mini lop rabbit may want to smell your hand. That is normal. If you hold the hand up, it might seem like a threat to the mini lop rabbit, who will think that you are going to strike him.

When you get close, your mini lop rabbit might try to bite you. The scent that you emit is one of the most important things for any pet. This is the first association with a human that the pet will make. So, be as calm as possible and make sure that you do not startle the animal.

Using your body language and words effectively

There are a few things that your rabbit will do that will help you to understand him and his moods better. Some may be signs of inviting you while others are telling you to back away.

For example, if he makes a nipping action with the mouth, this is a sign of warning. The rabbit is telling you that he does not approve of you being too close to him.

It is important that you understand his actions and moods when you are trying to train him. If you force him to learn something, you will only face disappointment. It is always better to give the rabbit some time and space. You will learn more about his actions as and when you spend more time with him.

If the rabbit is running around you and is trying to pull at your leg or pants, this means that the mini lop rabbit wants something that you have with you. If this habit is not stopped, it can lead to a painful bite in the future. You must stop this with a strong "No". The voice should be clear and loud.

If he rests his head on your foot or stands quietly next to you, this is a sign that the mini lop rabbit is very comfortable in your presence. This means that the pet is comfortable with you being around, which is a good sign.

If the pet turns his back on you each time you approach him, this is a sign that he is extremely nervous in your presence. When the rabbit does this, do not pet the animal. He might try to hurt you. This can lead to severe injuries if you get too close to the animal.

It is true that rabbits and many other animals do not respond first to verbal communication. The tone of your voice is very important and not so much the words that you use.

Keeping the tone uniform during a certain movement allows your rabbit to read what you and the action means. For instance, if you use the word "no" regularly in a certain tone, he understands that you are not pleased with something.

The pitch of the voice is important. If you keep the voice soft and low, it can have a rather calming effect on the rabbit. You should know that while words are not really a method of communicating with animals, the tone is universal.

However, without any control on your body language and the energy that you are sending out, the tone of your voice cannot help you much when it comes to dealing with these pets. The cues that you give to the animal are of utmost importance.

3. Litter training

As the owner, you are also the caretaker and the parent for the pet. You will have to teach him stuff that he needs to know when living in a family. Don't get upset when you see your rabbit littering all around. You can train him not to do so.

To begin with, you should buy a few litter boxes. Keep these boxes in various areas of the house where the rabbit is most likely to litter. You should cover the various corners where you have found the litter earlier. In addition, install one box in the cage. Eventually, you want the rabbit to litter in the cage itself.

It is believed that a mini lop rabbit will generally litter in the first fifteen or twenty minutes of waking up. So, there is a chance that the rabbit has already littered in the box in the cage. When you open the cage to take him out, check the box and wait until he has used the box.

You should signal the animal by pointing towards the litter box. The pet should slowly realize that he needs to use the box if he wants to get out of the cage. You should wait near the cage until he is all done.

Another point that you need to understand here is that rabbits are very smart. When the rabbit understands that you will let him out of the cage once he uses the litter box, he might pretend to use it. You need to check the box and make sure that he has actually used it.

If you notice that the pet is not using the litter box installed in his cage, then you need to understand why. There is a chance that the litter box is uncomfortable for him. In such a case, you should look to buy a box with a front ledge that is low. This is good for your rabbit.

You can even make one. If you buy a cat litter box, you will notice that the front ledge is not too low. You could cut it in half to make it suitable for your rabbit. The idea is to make it really comfortable for your pet rabbit. A suitable litter box will have a back ledge that is high. This gives the right support to the pet.

The rabbit will take its own time to adjust to the environment. It is always difficult for a new pet to adjust. If you get him a new cage or if you make any changes in his surroundings, he will find it difficult to adjust, but this problem is only time related and will get solved.

Every time the rabbit litters outside the box, place his litter in the box that he should be using. You need to show the pet that he should be using the litter box. This could be difficult for you in the beginning, but the rabbit will learn soon. You should place food and toys in areas and corners that you want to save.

When the rabbit sees a toy or a food item in a corner, he will try to look for another corner to pass his stool. You can also place a mat underneath the litter box to save your carpet or home mats. Make sure that the mat that you use is waterproof.

Observe your rabbit's mannerisms when he is using the litter box. If he has a tendency to bite the mat underneath or stuff kept around, you should discourage this behavior. To do so, you can use bitter food sprays on the mats and other stuff. This will automatically discourage the pet from biting around when he is littering.

The litter box of the rabbit should definitely be kept clean to maintain the overall hygiene and to prevent diseases. You should wash the box once a week. Yet, a point that needs to be noted here is that the box should not be too clean. A clean litter box that almost appears new could be appealing to you, but it is a turn off to the rabbit.

The rabbit will use its sense of smell to use the areas that he has used before. You should leave some paper litter in the box to encourage the pet to use the box again. This is a simple trick that you can use when you are trying to litter train your pet.

When you are buying a litter box, you should remember that the size of the box will depend on the size of your rabbit. For example, a male pet rabbit will need a bigger box due to his size compared to the box that a female pet rabbit will need.

If you are domesticating more than one rabbit in your home, then this will also affect the littering process of the rabbits. This may come as a surprise to you, but the dominant pet could affect how the other pets use the litter boxes in the house.

You might notice that the habits of a dominant pet rabbit are influencing the other pet rabbits. The dominant one will always try to boss around and make the others feel inferior.

Rabbits don't like to use the same litter box. The rabbits could also be competing for a litter box. These are the issues that you will have to find out. Observe which rabbit is using which litter box and which one suddenly leaves a litter box.

You should make sure that each rabbit has his own box, so that he not left to use the carpets and the floor. Even after you have trained your rabbit to use the litter box, you have to be vigilant.

If you are observant, you might face issues. There could be instances when your pet would suddenly give up the use of the litter box. Instead of getting angry at him, it is important that you probe into the reason for his sudden change in behavior.

When the pet is sick, he might give up the use of the litter box. The main reason behind this is that the pet might not have the strength in his hind legs to get on to the box. He could be suffering from a gastro intestinal or adrenal disease, which could make him weak and lethargic.

You should be cautious when you observe such changes in your pet rabbit. Don't ignore his condition, or don't force him to use the litter box. You should not get angry with the pet because he is littering on the floor. It is not his fault if he is not well.

The best thing to do in such a situation is to take the pet to the vet. This will prevent the condition getting worse. He/she will look for the symptoms of various diseases and will help you to understand what is wrong with the pet.

The given process will take some days, but you will have to have some patience. The idea is to help the pet get used to the food before you can expect the pet to eat the food. Once he gets used to it, he will try out the food item on his own.

4. Training the pet against chewing and biting

When you buy a new mini lop rabbit, you might notice that the animal has a tendency to bite things. This is a very natural behaviour of a rabbit. They try to bite and chew everything. So, you shouldn't be very surprised.

You will see him trying to chew everything he can, such as furniture and plants. He will not even hesitate to chew wires, which can be very harmful for him. This is the reason why the rabbit needs to be supervised.

As an owner this can be uncomfortable and worrisome for you. But, you should know that this is absolutely normal for the bunny and that you can slowly train the mini lop rabbit not to exhibit such behaviour. You can teach him not to bite you and other members.

The first and foremost thing that you should remember is that you should not harm the pet when he tries to bite you. This could scare him and will make things worse for you. The pet needs to be handled with care if you wish to teach him the right behaviour in the household.

If you mishandle the pet and try to beat him up, he might also try to bite and harm you. Avoid going this road and aim at training the mini lop rabbit well.

It is important that you understand the reason behind the mini lop rabbit's biting. More often than not, mini lop rabbits do so when they are in a playful mood.

If the mini lop rabbit wants you to play with him, he could just signal you to do so by chewing. Such behaviour is quite common in younger mini lop rabbits.

Another reason behind a mini lop rabbit's nipping is that the animal could be scared. When you bring the pet to your home for the first time, everything around him will be new. It is quite natural for the pet to get scared. This is the reason that chewing and biting is very common in a new pet mini lop rabbit.

When you know what you can expect from a new pet, it gets easier. Try to understand that he is still uncomfortable in the new surroundings and will require some time to get used to all that is new around him. Give him that space, time and also your understanding.

Biting comes very naturally to the mini lop rabbits. But, this does not harm them because of the quality of their skin. If you notice the skin of your pet, you will find it to be thick. This thick skin is a cushion for the mini lop rabbit.

The mini lop rabbit might be happy and playful, but his chewing and biting will hurt you, so it is important to train him against such behaviour.

As explained earlier, a mini lop rabbit can exhibit such behaviour when they are scared. It should be noted that if the mini lop rabbit has had a history of abuse then you can expect him to chew and bite more in fear than in a playful mood.

If the mini lop rabbit bites you real hard you can have a really bad wound. This makes it all the more important to train the pet. There are many mini lop rabbits that are beaten up and abused. If you have rescued one such animal, then you will definitely find him trying to bite you out of fear and tension.

But, don't worry because this is a passing phase. The love and warmth he will get at your place will help him to come out of his history of beatings and abuse.

If the pet is very young, he needs to be taught the behaviour that is expected of him. He needs to learn to be sociable. He needs to learn that it is not okay to bite people. There are some tips and tricks that will help you to teach him all this.

Every time the pet tries to bite you, you should loudly say the word 'no'. Do it each time, till the mini lop rabbit starts relating the word 'no' to something that he can't do. Don't beat him because this will only scare him. Just be stern with your words and also actions.

If you think that the above trick is not very useful, then you can put the pet in his cage for some time. The pet will eventually understand that this behaviour will send him into the cage. The word 'no' and the act of putting him into the cage will make the pet more cautious of his behaviour.

It should be noted that it will take some time for the mini lop rabbit to understand this. Until then just be patient and keep repeating these actions each time he tries to nip you. The mini lop rabbit will call back on his memory eventually and relate the cage to something punishable.

Another trick to help the mini lop rabbit understand that he can't nip and bite is to hold him and drag him away from you. You need to establish the fact that you are the dominant one in the house.

When you are pulling the mini lop rabbit away, you need to be very careful. You want to train the pet and not harm him. Use your thumb and the index finger to hold the skin at the back of the mini lop rabbit's neck. This skin is loose and you will be able to hold it easily.

Look for the reactions of the mini lop rabbit. He should not be in pain. The idea is to teach him to give up nipping and biting. When you hold him at the back of his neck, gently push him away from you.

You might have to repeat this action several times before the mini lop rabbit understands what is expected of him. The mini lop rabbit might also try to give you a good fight when you pull him away.

Don't worry because this is something normal and quite natural of the mini lop rabbit. The mini lop rabbits play and fight amongst themselves in the natural environment, so he might just try to defend and play with you.

There is another trick that can definitely help your training sessions with the mini lop rabbit. You can apply something bitter on your toes and fingers, so that when the mini lop rabbit bites you, he gets that bitter taste. When he gets to taste something bitter and terrible on you, he will eventually give up on nipping you.

It is important that the food item that you use is bitter but is not harmful for the mini lop rabbit. You should know that there are some specially designed bitter foods for the mini lop rabbits. These food items are prepared keeping in mind the training of the pet mini lop rabbits.

You can easily buy these bitter food products online. You can also buy such products from the stores that have rabbit and bunny related stuff. You can buy various bitter products, such as bitter apple and bitter lemon.

These products are extremely safe for the mini lop rabbit, so you can use them without any doubts. They render the bitter taste that will disgust the mini lop rabbit. You just need to apply them or spray them to your toes and tips of the fingers. While you are working hard to train your pet mini lop rabbit well, you should remember that you don't want to do anything that is not right for the pet in the long run.

For example, if you use too much of these bitter food products, the digestive system of the nini lop rabbit can get upset. You just need to spray a little. This will be enough to get the job done and also not affect the mini lop rabbit in a negative way. He just needs a little to get the bitter taste in his mouth.

After your pet has tasted the bitter product and is disgusted, you need to make it up to him. Wash off your hands and toes nicely and give the pet a treat. This is important so that the pet is not scared of you and your hands. This will also make him realize that nipping is not accepted, but eating from your hands is.

There are many treats that the mini lop rabbit can lick. You can find these treats online. You can also treat your pet to these foods, so that he can affectionately lick from your hands. You should remember that the mini lop rabbit will start ignoring and avoiding you if he only gets to taste bitter stuff from you. Be a teacher to the pet, but remember to be a friendly teacher.

Another point that you need to know while training your pet is that you need to monitor your actions too. You need to figure out whether biting is a habit with the pet or has he suddenly started. If the pet has recently started biting, then it could be something related to you.

Another reason that could be behind your mini lop rabbit's biting is that the mini lop rabbit is sick. You have to know your pet well to be able to detect sudden changes in his behaviour. If you see the pet being aggressive when you try to play with him, he could be sick.

You should thoroughly examine your pet for any injuries. If you spot an injury, you should take him to the veterinarian. If he looks sick and tired, even then it is a good idea to take him to the veterinarian. You should never postpone such things because this will drastically affect the pet's health.

5. Teaching the bunny some fun tricks and games

As the prospective owner of the mini lop rabbit, you will be delighted to know that you can teach your pet mini lop rabbit some fun games and tricks.

The way you can train your mini lop rabbit for various essential things, you can also train them to understand some of your tricks. For example, the animal can be trained to know that he is being called.

You can teach him to associate certain actions with certain words. There are many other fun tricks that will help you bond with your pet. These tricks are also very entertaining. Your family and friends will surely have a great time when you and your pet do your fun tricks.

Like any other training, even these fun tricks will take some time. You will have to be patient with your pet if you want him to understand your commands well. There are some easy and fun tips that will make this process entertaining.

There are many tricks that you can teach the mini lop rabbit. You can teach him to roll on the floor. Similarly, you can teach him to run around your feet when you command him to.

You can give a healthy treat to the pet when he is able to follow your instructions. The idea is to repeat a set of instructions and help him do an action.

Give him a treat when he does it right. This will help him to understand what is required of him. Treats are simple way of making the pets do what you want them to do.

In the beginning, you will have to repeat the set of instructions again and again. But, with the passage of time, your aim should be to reduce the number of times the instructions need to be repeated.

The pet bunny should be able to associate a set of words to an action. You should also not make him too dependent on the treats. This is not a very healthy thing to do.

It can be very difficult if the bunny hides and refuses to budge. Don't force him and give him some time. The mini lop rabbits will follow your lead and will have fun with you, but you need to be a little patient with them.

A simple trick that you can try to make your pet bunny listen to you is to give him a special treat. All animals love treats. When he will see this favourite food item in your hand, he will get all excited.

When you bring the treat near him, take the treat upwards. The mini lop rabbit will try to reach the treat, and in this process will stand on the hind legs.

Next, lower the treat towards the ground. The movement of the treat in your hand will also inspire the movement of the bunny. Do it every time you give him the treat.

You can also say the word dance when you move the treat upwards and downwards. The mini lop rabbit will slowly realize that to eat the treat he will have to stand on the hind legs and then sit back.

Make sure you do this only for fun and not to trouble your pet mini lop rabbit. Once you and your pet are good with the trick, you can flaunt and boast in front of your family and friends that you can make the pet perform tricks.

You can also teach your rabbit to do a certain action for you. But, this will take a lot of time and patience from you. For example, you can teach the pet to perform a roll over for you on the ground.

Lay the pet mini lop bunny on the ground, say the words roll over loud and clear and then give the pet a gentle roll over with your palm. Repeat this action many times. This will teach the pet that he needs to roll over.

The pet will start associating the word roll over with a roll over on the ground. When you say roll over, he will start rolling over on the ground on his own. This might take many days, even weeks of practice, so be prepared.

Also, if your pet seems uncomfortable with you rolling him over, you should just quit. Some bunnies might feel a little vulnerable with such an action. Understand your bunny's reactions and then take the next step.

These tricks and games can be very entertaining for everybody who gets to watch these tricks. Mini lop rabbits are anyways very entertaining and when you apply these simple tricks with them, they become more playful.

Chapter 8: Grooming and showing the mini lop rabbit

It is important to groom a mini lop rabbit in order to ensure that the coat stays smooth and shiny and the pet stays in the best of health. If you plan to enter your pet bunny into shows, grooming is particularly important. You will have to dedicate time for grooming sessions in order to keep the pet clean and healthy.

1. Grooming the mini lop rabbit

You should understand that when you pay attention to the basic cleaning and grooming of the pet rabbit, not only will your pet appear neat and clean; he will also be saved from many unwanted diseases.

When you are looking at grooming sessions for your rabbit, you should pay special attention to the pet's ears, nails, coat, teeth and bathing. This chapter will help you to understand the various dos and don'ts while grooming your pet mini lop rabbit.

It should be noted here that the mini lop rabbit will not require frequent bathing, but regular brushing of the coat is important to keep the wool in good condition. If you fail to groom the pet regularly, you will put the wool and the skin of the pet at risk.

If you are domesticating the rabbit for its wool or for showing the rabbit, then it is very important that you groom the pet nicely. Grooming the pet rabbit is also necessary to maintain the hygiene and well being of the pet. Even if the pet will not participate in shows, you should make sure that he is neat and clean at all times.

Most rabbits are easy to handle. This nature of the pet makes it very simple for the caregiver to groom the pet. However, you should understand that much will depend on the individual personality of your pet.

You should start the grooming sessions with the pet when he is very young. When you start a grooming session with the adult rabbit, he might take some time to get used to the new routine.

On the other hand, if you start when the pet is very young, you give him some time to get accustomed to frequent grooming sessions. This is good for you and the pet in the long run.

You should take special care of the mini lop rabbit's wool. The wool needs to be combed regularly to maintain the health and luster of the same. If you don't comb it regularly, you will see the wool getting tangled.

Once the wool is tangled, it can be a real pain for you to get rid of these tangles. You will have to apply pressure and force, which can be very uncomfortable and painful for the pet rabbit.

It is important to note that this can cause the bunny to shed loose tendril of its wool. This is a warning signal for you as the caregiver of the pet that something is not right with the health of the rabbit.

Mini lop rabbits have the tendency to groom themselves. They will lick themselves like cats. This can cause the bunny to swallow some of the hair or wool. The rabbit is unable to cough this ball of hair like cats do.

This can lead to a serious health issue called wool block. The hairball remains inside the pet's body in this condition. This can lead to many complications if the condition is not treated on time.

The rabbit feels that his stomach is full because of the presence of a hairball in his stomach. This makes him lose his appetite and he eats less. This can be really detrimental for the overall health of the pet rabbit.

It should be noted that this condition is rare in mini lop rabbits, but still you need to be prepared.

You should help your pet in this condition by feeding large quantities of hay because it has fiber. You should also make sure that the pet rabbit drinks a lot of water to help him during this condition.

Cleaning the ears

It should be noted that while certain rabbits are prone to various kinds of ear infections, many others aren't. The rabbits with erect ears are less prone to such infections. On the other hand, smaller ears that are not open are more prone to ear infections.

An erect ear type gets enough airflow to save it from infections. Mini lop rabbits have erect ears. Their ears are open and allow good airflow. While the design of the ears help the mini lop rabbit to ward off infections, you also need to do your bit.

It should be noted that wet ears are susceptible to bacteria. The bacteria can grow in the ear and lead to various diseases.

The ears of the mini lop rabbit also need to be cleaned regularly so that there is no wax deposited in the ears. There are many owners who might not consider ear cleaning an important part of pet keeping, but in reality wax can lead to mite infestation and other infections.

In severe cases, the hearing power of the pet can be compromised. It is important that you know of the early signs of mite infestation. The wax in the ears will have a light brown color, while the wax with mites will be dark brown in color.

It is important to see the veterinarian in case you have doubts about mite infestations. Don't put any drops in the pet's ears without consulting the vet. In general, you should try to clean the pet's ears once a week, or at least once in ten days.

You will require a cotton swab and an ear cleaning solution that is used for rabbits. If there is somebody in the house who could help you, it will be easier to clean the ears.

If you are the only one doing this task, you should be calm and patient because mini lop rabbits don't like their ears being touched and cleaned. You can warm the cleaning solution before use.

Sit comfortably on the floor and hold the mini lop rabbit gently by the loose skin behind the neck. Use your lap to give support to the pet's legs. Take a cotton swab and apply some cleaning agent to it.

You should use the cotton swab with the cleaning agent to clean the parts of the ear that are easily visible to you. Don't go too deep because this can hurt the pet. You should definitely not try to go further in the ear canal.

Repeat the process on both the ears. If you commit a small mistake from your side, it could cost the mini lop rabbit his hearing. So, you need to make sure that whatever you do is gentle, yet with firm hands.

The mini lop rabbit might get uneasy and might try to get away from your grip. To make sure that the pet is stable and not jerking, you can give him a treat. This will keep him occupied and will make your job easier.

Trimming the nails

It is important to cut the nails of the mini lop rabbit regularly. You should be looking at doing so at least once a month. If the nails of the mini lop rabbit are not cut on a regular basis, there is a chance that the nails will get stuck somewhere. This will cause the nails to get uprooted.

You can imagine the pain your mini lop rabbit will have to go through if the nails are uprooted. You will have to rush to the veterinarian to help the mini lop rabbit. Not only this, but the long nails can also leave marks and scratches on your skin. So, make it a point to cut the nails of the pet regularly.

You should also make sure that you use the right equipment to cut the nails of the pet mini lop rabbit. You should use good quality animal nail clippers. Along with that, you would need soap and styptic powder.

You can give some treats to the pet rabbit. This is to distract the animal so that he does not disturb you when you are busy clipping his nails.

If there is someone else in the house, you can ask them to hold the mini lop rabbit. If you're on your own, place the mini lop rabbit in your lap in a way that he is comfortable and you have access to his nails.

You will notice a reddish vein on the nail. This is called the quick. You should cut the nail in a way that the quick is not touched. If you happen to cut it, it will hurt the pet and will also bleed.

In case you cut the nail in way that the quick starts bleeding, use soap to clean it and then apply the powder. This will give relief to the pet. You should give a few minutes for the mini lop rabbit to feel better before starting the process of clipping the nails once again.

Cleaning the teeth

Taking care of the teeth is an important part of grooming the mini lop rabbit. As the owner of the mini lop rabbit, it is important for you to know that the teeth of the rabbit are always growing. If you pay attention you will realize that the teeth sometimes become so big that the rabbit has difficulties in eating.

When you are considering the overall hygiene and cleanliness of the mini lop rabbit, you also have to take care of his teeth. You might have problems cleaning the pet mini lop rabbit's teeth in the beginning, but he will get used it quickly.

As a rule, you should try to clean the mini lop rabbit's teeth once or twice a month. If you ignore his teeth, you will only invite unwanted problems for the mini lop rabbit. You will notice tar depositing on the teeth if they are not clean. This will automatically lead to tooth decay.

Many owners complain that the pet closes its mouth while the teeth are being cleaned. This makes it very difficult for the cleaning to take place. If your pet does this, then you can clean only one side of the mouth in one sitting. This means that you will have to be more frequent with the teeth cleaning sessions.

It is also important that you take the pet to the vet if you see any tar on the teeth. Even if all seems fine, it is advised to schedule dental check-ups for the mini lop rabbit once or twice a year. The vet will trim the teeth of the pet if there is a need.

To keep the teeth clean on a regular basis, you can find toothpaste specially designed for rabbits. Along with the toothpaste, you should use a soft brush that has been specially designed for them. A toothbrush with hard bristles might hurt the pet's jaw, so you should avoid using it.

Your movements should be very soft. If you are too hard, you will hurt the mini lop rabbit. Be very observant of the lather that comes out from the pet's mouth. If you see a pink or red color, you should immediately know that it is blood and that you are being too hard on the bunny's mouth.

Brushing the coat

It should be noted that brushing the coat of the mini lop rabbit is essential. You should make sure that you brush the coat of the animal regularly. This will help to ease out the tangles in the hairs of the rabbit.

Regular brushing of the coat will also help you to get rid of dust from the coat. This is important to keep the mini lop rabbit neat and clean. You need a brush with soft bristles. Hard bristles can harm the pet, so avoid such a brush. You can buy a good brush online at a cheap price or from a local pet shop near your area.

Mini lop rabbits have short coats. You need to brush the coat regularly to avoid any fur balls. If you are regular in brushing your rabbit's coat, you automatically eliminate the need to bathe him on a regular basis.

Bathing the mini lop rabbit

Mini lop rabbits belong to the class of animals that are not extremely fond of bathing. However, the good news is that these animals do not require regular bathing. There are a few species of rabbits that need to be bathed every now and then, but your mini lop rabbit does not.

Though the pet does not require regular baths, it is important that you understand the circumstances under which the pet should be bathed. You should also lay emphasis on how the bath should be given. It is important that the pet is handled with care and love. Don't be forceful and have some patience with the animal.

Bathing is known to be a very stressful event for mini lop rabbits. They don't take it well. They also take a lot of time to dry. The wet coat can actually lead to diseases such as pneumonia.

However, this does not mean that the pet should be left dirty. If the pet is not clean, he will attract fleas and other parasites. This only means extra work for you and veterinarian visits for the rabbit. Make sure that the pet is well groomed to avoid such hassles.

The frequency of a bath should depend on the climate and the environment of the bunny. If it is too hot or if the surroundings are not too clean, it means that your pet should be given a bath more often than a bunny that resides in cleaner and cooler environments.

Sometimes, a veterinarian will advise you to bathe the mini lop rabbit. This could be to cool his body and to lower his fever, if he is sick. Schedule a bath once every few weeks. The rest of the time you can use wet wipes to clean the rabbit of any dirt or dust.

Bathing is also important to keep the coat of the rabbit clean. This is important to maintain good quality wool of the pet. If you don't clean the coat, the rabbit gets prone to many skin diseases.

If the rabbit is shedding its wool tendrils, the excess wool might stick on to the body. When you give the pet a bath, the loose tendrils will just get washed off with water. This also means that the fur will not be shed all over the house.

When you are looking to give a nice bath to your rabbit, you should be looking at two things: a good quality and mild shampoo and a few towels. It is very important that you choose the right shampoo for the mini lop rabbit.

If the shampoo is too hard or harsh, it will leave rashes on the rabbit and might even cause serious damage to his skin. This makes it important that you invest in buying a mild shampoo.

You can easily get a good quality shampoo online or in the pet store. Make sure that the shampoo that you choose is very mild on the skin and has proven to be ideal for the mini lop rabbit.

You can take a small amount of shampoo and test it on a small part of the skin of the rabbit. This is to make sure that the shampoo is safe for the pet. If you see the skin reacting, then you should make sure that you avoid this shampoo.

You also need a few towels handy for the mini lop rabbit. They will help to dry the wool of the pet nicely.

There are a few precautions that you need to take. You should understand that how your rabbit behaves in water will depend on its individual personality. It is important that you make a few attempts to understand your pet's personality. Don't give up and understand his behavior and mannerisms. This will only help you in your future dealings with the pet.

You should always remember that while it is fine to bathe the rabbit once in a while, over-bathing is not recommended. This can also create many problems. The skin of the pet will begin to lose many important essential oils if they are bathed frequently.

If your mini lop rabbit is suffering from flea infestation, then you will have to use a shampoo that can help the mini lop rabbit get rid of the fleas. You should consult the veterinarian before you use a specialized flea shampoo. It is important not to take a chance on the health of the pet.

It is important that you make a few attempts to understand your pet's personality. Don't give up and understand his behavior and mannerisms. This will only help you in your future dealings with the pet.

To begin with, make sure that the water you are using to bathe the pet is warm. Mini lop rabbits can get stressed very easily. They will detest cold water. They should be bathed in warm water to keep them safe.

Take a tub and fill it half with warm water. Lift your mini lop rabbit delicately in your hands. Make sure that your grip is firm. The pet might surprise you when it touches water and might try to jump out of your hands. To avoid such a situation, place your hands on the stomach area and hold him firmly.

Place the mini lop rabbit in the tub of warm water for a few seconds. Observe how he responds to water. If you see him enjoying, then your work becomes easier. You can also sprinkle water over the pet. But, if the pet is not enjoying then you need to be quick.

Take him out of the water, and put some shampoo on his back. You should form a good lather with your hands from the ears towards the tail region. Make sure that the pet does not escape when you are shampooing it. You need to have a firm grip on him.

You can also make use of the kitchen sink to give the rabbit a bath. The sink will be deep and it will be difficult for the bunny to run away. The pet is hydrophobic, so it is advised to use to two sinks or tubs. Fill both with water and use them alternately. Keep talking to your pet and make him feel that everything is fine.

Another way to bathe your hydrophobic mini lop rabbit is to sway him under running warm water. Turn the tap on and make sure the water is warm. It should not be cold or too hot. Once you are convinced that the temperature of the water is right for the pet, hold the pet and bring him under the water for a few seconds.

Before he starts to get fidgety, take him away from the water. Now apply some shampoo over the mini lop rabbit. Keeping swaying him under the water until all the shampoo is washed off. It is very important that all the shampoo is washed off; else the pet's skin will get affected and will show signs of rashes and abrasions.

After the bath is done, place the bunny in a big towel. You should place a few blankets or towels on the floor to keep it warm and tight for the animal. The mini lop rabbit will show too much energy at this time. He will try to escape you. You should be very gentle with the pet, otherwise you could harm him.

While you are bathing the mini lop rabbit, it is important that you protect his face. Water should not enter his eyes or ears. These are sensitive areas and water could cause some damage to them. Keep him on the towels and use another towel to pat him dry. Make sure that he is absolutely dry before you let him go, otherwise he will stick dust and dirt on his skin.

Giving a full bath to the mini lop rabbit is not an easy job. While it is difficult, it is also not very good for the pet. The pet can get dry skin, which can further lead to many skin related problems and other diseases.

More often than not, the pet owner is forced to give a bath to the mini lop rabbit because he has soiled his feet or coat. If you don't clean the feet, the mini lop rabbit can soil other areas and can also get an infection.

If you are trying to get rid of this problem, then you can give a footbath instead of a full bath. For a simple footbath, fill a water tub or sink with over half an inch of water. Make the pet walk in the tub or sink. This will help him to get rid of the poopy boots.

You can also wet a big towel or a paper towel and make the mini lop rabbit walk on it. You can also use baby wipes if you want to get rid of dirt or a little amount of grime. This is a simple way to avoid a full bath. You can also use these baby wipes to clean off the dirt from this skin and coat.

2. Showing the mini lop rabbits

Mini lop rabbits are adorable pets, but they are capable of being more than just household pets. There are many owners that keep and domesticate mini lop rabbits to make them take part in shows. These shows are extensively popular amongst many rabbit lovers.

If you also wish to keep or domesticate the mini lop rabbit for the purpose of showing, then you need to make sure that you follow certain guidelines. There are certain breed standards that your mini lop rabbit needs to qualify for.

The American Rabbit Breeders Association (ARBA) has set some guidelines that will help you to prepare your mini lop rabbits to participate in such shows. You should make sure that you understand these guidelines. These guidelines will help you not just in preparing your rabbit for the show, but also to take good care of the pet.

Rabbit shows give you the opportunity to showcase your rabbit and also win a potential prize. These shows will also help you to meet other rabbit owners. You can connect and exchange notes about your pet animals. This is a great opportunity to broaden your horizons and know more about your breed of rabbit and also other breeds.

It should be noted that you can't suddenly wake up from a slumber and decide to participate in shows. Even if you do so, you will not gain much from the shows. If you are serious about showing your rabbit, then you will have to prepare all year round.

You need to take proper care of the rabbit. You will have to make sure that everything about the bunny is on point. There are many people who take rabbit shows very seriously. They prepare religiously for them. So, it is advised that you prepare well or just quit participating in such rabbit shows.

This chapter will help you understand some breed standards for the mini lop rabbits. You will understand how to keep and present the pet in the best possible way. Certain tips for the shows will also be shared. You will learn what needs to be done before the show and on the day of the show.

Breed standards for the mini lop rabbits

The BRC has set total 100 points for judging mini lop rabbits. Out of these 100 points, 30 points are for body, 15 points for ears, 15 points for head, 5 points for eyes, 15 points for color, 10 points for coat and 10 points are for the condition of the rabbit.

The BRC also has the right to disqualify your rabbit from the rabbit show. The rabbit can be disqualified if it is not healthy or is overdeveloped for its age. It can also be disqualified if it has crooked legs, runny eyes, mutilated teeth, odd color, putty nose, white patches and white armpits.

Preparing for the show

You need to be a member of an organization. The ARBA organization and BRC organization are the two organizations that will allow you to be a member and also enter a show with your mini lop rabbit. You can register with either of the two organizations.

The process to become a member is fairly simple and straightforward. You need to approach the organization and show an interest in being their member. You should also register your pet under your mini lop rabbit name.

Once you are a member of the organization, you will be intimated with all the latest happenings and shows in your area. You should be alert regarding the requirements and deadlines. The registration process can take some time, so don't wait until the last minute to get it done.

If you want to enter a show with your mini lop rabbit, you will have to make sure that your rabbit is in its best form. You should take care of the health and well being of the animal and make sure that he is ready for the contest.

After you are sure that your rabbit is ready to take part in the contest, you can plan on getting him admitted for the show. Always keep checks on the shows happening in your area. You should check if your rabbit fits the requirements.

When you find a show that allows your breed of rabbit to take part in the contest, you should go ahead and register your rabbit. Register your rabbit in the show that you find relevant and suitable.

Though most rules are quite standard, it is always advised to be careful so that your rabbit is not disqualified from the show or subsequent shows. You should also note the deadlines related to the application and other things. It is always better to be prepared before the main show day.

Once you have registered for the show, you need to make sure that you and the pet are ready. Make all the necessary arrangements to get to the venue much before the final day.

After the rabbit is registered to participate in the rabbit show, the wait for the final day begins. You have to ensure that you have all the necessary documents and a copy of the exact schedule with you. You should know the exact time when your bunny would be showed. Having these things handy will help you to avoid the last minute rush and tension.

Final show day

There is nothing much that you need to do from your side on the day of the show. It is advised to take the opportunity and observe other bunnies. This will help you to understand mini lop rabbits in a better light. This will go on to help you to take better care of your pet rabbit.

While you have done your part for the preparation for the show, there are a few pointers that will help on the final day of the rabbit show. This section will help you to understand the procedure of judging the rabbits on the day of the show. It is important not to panic and to understand things well. It is just a show. You need to learn from it and also enjoy it.

When you apply for the show, you will be told by the organizers whether your rabbit qualifies for the show or not. You need not worry, as you will get plenty of time to prepare for the main event. While you are taking good care of the pet mini lop rabbit and preparing well for the rabbit show, you should also prepare a handy kit. This kit will help you on the day of the show. Your kit should have all the items that the bunny or you might need on the final day of the show.

You should securely keep the registration form of the pet in the kit. You will need to show it at the venue. You should keep your business card with the form. Make sure that you keep a towel, some paper wipes, nail clippers and a slicker brush. You can also keep scrap carpet squares and hydrogen peroxide for emergency grooming and cleaning of the bunny.

It is also a good idea to keep a collapsible stool. This will be essential when you know that chairs won't be available. You should also keep some fresh food and water for the bunny on the day of the show. Apart from packing the essentials for the rabbit, don't forget to carry food and water for you. You need to take care of yourself so that you can take care of the rabbit.

After your rabbit has been confirmed for the main show, you will be told about the start time of the show and the time of judging the rabbits. You will also be assigned a pen by the organizers. You are supposed to keep the rabbit ready to be judged in the assigned pen. It is always better to reach the venue earlier. Once you reach the venue, look for the assigned pen for your bunny.

If you wish to understand the procedure of these rabbit shows then you should know that the process of the judging in a rabbit show is quite simple. It is same across all competitions. The judges will visit all the pens one by one. They will judge the bunnies on various parameters, such as coat health, eyes and ears.

You are not expected to do much when the rabbit is in the competition ready to be judged. You should relax and enjoy the show. You should just make sure that the rabbit is in the pen at the time of judging. The last thing that you want is your rabbit sneaking out at the time of judgment. A bunny that is not in the pen will obviously not be judged.

After all the rabbits are evaluated, the judges will exchange notes and announce the winners of the show. The winners would be chosen keeping in mind all the parameters set for the competition.

If your rabbit wins a prize, a card will be left by the judges on the pen your pet rabbit is in. Once the entire process is over, you can take the card and get the equivalent prize money from the reception area.

Once you get your prize money, you are free to leave the rabbit show. If you wish to, you can also spend more time and connect with other owners. You can share notes with these owners. Irrespective of the result of the show, you should make sure that you make the most of this opportunity. You can discuss your issues and doubts regarding the pet with other owners.

It is always a good idea to learn from the experience of other people. These rabbit shows allow you to do so. You can also help other owners learn from your own experience. This is a great way to form a close-knit community of rabbit owners that can help each other.

Conclusion

Thank you again for purchasing this book!

I hope this book was able to help you in understanding the various ways to domesticate and care for mini lop rabbits.

Mini lop rabbits are adorable and lovable animals. These animals have been domesticated for many years. Even though they are loved as pets, they are not very common, and there are still many doubts regarding their domestications methods and techniques. There are many things that prospective owners don't understand about the animal. They find themselves getting confused as to what should be done and what should be avoided.

A mini lop rabbit is a small, naughty animal that will keep you busy and entertained by all its unique antics and mischiefs. It is said that each animal is different. Each one will have some traits that are unique to him. It is important to understand the traits that differentiate the mini lop rabbit from other animals. You also have to be sure that you can provide for the animal. So, it is important to be acquainted with the dos and don'ts of keeping the mini lop rabbit.

When you decide to domesticate an animal, it is important that you understand the animal and its species well. It is important to learn the basic nature and mannerisms of the animal. This book will help you to equip yourself with this knowledge. You will be able to appreciate a mini lop rabbit for what it is. You will also know what to expect from the animal. This will help you to decide whether the mini lop rabbit is the right choice for you or not. If you already have a mini lop rabbit, then this book will help you to strengthen your bond with your pet.

The ways and strategies discussed in the book are meant to help you get acquainted with everything that you need to know about mini lop rabbits. You will be able to understand the unique antics of the animal. This will help you to decide whether the mini lop rabbit is suitable to be your pet. The book teaches you simple ways that will help you to understand your pet.

Thank you and good luck!

References

Note: at the time of printing, all the websites below were working. As the internet changes rapidly, some sites might no longer be live when you read this book. That is, of course, out of our control.

http://www.nationalgeographic.com

http://www.runningbugfarm.com

http://joyofhandspinning.com

http://www.rabbit.org

http://www.mnn.com

http://www.handallhousefarm.com

http://twotalentshomestead.blogspot.in

https://hub.co-opinsurance.co.uk

https://www.popsugar.com

http://ipfactly.com

https://www.petcha.com

http://www.petrabbitinfo.com

https://www.peta2.com

http://www.raising-rabbits.com

http://www.petguide.com

https://joybileefarm.com

https://www.thespruce.com

http://www.hobbyfarms.com

www.training.ntwc.org

http://animaldiversity.org

http://www.businessinsider.com

Printed in Great Britain
by Amazon